Hourly Prayer from Scripture Alone

A Week of 12 Hours Days

Plus 4 Night Watches

Compiled, translated, and edited by Matthew Bryan

Evening and morning and noon
I will pray and cry out,
and he will hear my voice.

Let my mouth be filled with praise,
so that I would sing your glory,
your majesty the whole day.

Contents

Introduction

This collection of prayers is not a to-do list to be completed each day. It offers not a rule of how and when to pray, but an aid for prayer. These prayers should not replace spontaneous praying, but serve as kindling wood for the fire.

"Faith comes by hearing, and hearing by the Word of the Lord," so the reader is encouraged to pray these passages aloud. Verbalized prayers encourage the heart and help us persevere in prayer by stopping the mind from drifting off into random thoughts.

Where the Psalmist prays about God's temple and God's house or "courts," such phrases now find fulfillment in hearts rather than buildings. Those who have become temples of the Holy Spirit now rejoice at the miracle of worshipping from within the innermost chambers of the heart.

When the Psalmist asks God for revenge or destruction of enemies, Christians redirect such requests toward our demonic enemies because "we wrestle not with flesh and blood."

Source:

Each word in this volume has been translated from either the Greek New Testament or the prophetic Jewish translation of the Old Testament into a Greek version called the

"Septuagint." This Jewish Septuagint version of the Psalms will present new words and phrases to those who are familiar with English translations of the Hebrew Old Testament. This prayer book uses the Septuagint version because it is the most popular source for quotations in the New Testament. More than 100 New Testament quotes of the Old Testament come from either a distinctly Hebrew or distinctly Greek version of the Jewish Scriptures. Only two of those New Testament quotations reflect the Hebrew version of the Old Testament, leaving more than 98% of such passages as coming from the Jewish Greek translation.

In the early centuries of Christianity, many leaders including Irenaeus, Justin Martyr, Origen, Epiphanius, and Augustine referred to the Septuagint as superior to the original Hebrew Old Testament. For example, Bishop Irenaeus, who was a direct disciple of one of the Apostle John's disciples, said that the Septuagint had the same divine inspiration as the original words of the prophets and the apostles of the Lord Jesus. Irenaeus said the Spirit of God "translated through the elders" the Jewish Greek Septuagint:

> *Thus it is the same Spirit of God who spoke through the prophets of the coming of the Lord, who properly translated through the elders what was really prophesied and*

Introduction

*who preached the fulfilment of the
promise through the apostles.*[1]

Such early Christians leaders believed that the Holy Spirit inspired the differences in the Greek translation as a preparation for the arrival of the Anointed King and the gospel of his kingdom. If these leaders were correct in their belief, then that would explain why New Testament quotations of Old Testament prophecies point to Jesus in a clearer manner than how the same read in Hebrew.

The most famous difference between the Hebrew Old Testament and the Jewish Greek translation might be the prophecy of the virgin birth of our Lord, where the original Hebrew only referred to a "maiden" but the Jewish Greek refers to a "virgin" in Isaiah 7:14. While the apostles of our Lord showed preference for the Greek Old Testament, the early church did not disdain the Hebrew. Irenaeus, for example, quoted both the Hebrew of Isaiah 9:6 and the Jewish Greek of its equivalent, Isaiah 9:5. The text of these two versions vary considerably, but Irenaeus treated both as divinely inspired.

Format:

Psalms make up the majority of this volume, and specific passages were selected based on whether they were amenable to Christian prayer. Prayers of the New Testament also appear, plus verses about prayer and some of King Jesus' teachings. Finally, some of the New Testament's confessions of faith are included, often as excerpts of verses rather than entire verses. Several passages regarding the Holy Spirit are also compiled here to emphasize our reliance on the Holy Spirit for prayer.

Wherever the Hebrew version of the Psalms employs the Name of God, this volume uses the capitalized English expression of "LORD." The beginning of each verse has been capitalized, regardless of whether it starts a new sentence. The beginning of a sentence will not be capitalized unless the first word coincides with the beginning of a verse or the beginning of a quoted statement like the statement quoted in Masoretic Psalm 27:8.

Quotation marks do not appear in this text, and divine pronouns are not capitalized. The Old English pronoun "ye" is occassionally used in this text to reflect the plural of "you," but no other Old English pronouns are employed.

In Masoretic Psalm 119 (which is numbered 118 in the Septuagint) the Psalmist used the Hebrew alphabet in stanzas of eight verses for each letter. Here the sound of those Hebrew letters will be favored for each of those sections where that sound can be used appropriately in English, with an emphasis on the first word of the first line of each stanza.

While it may seem trivial to avoid conventional names for the days of the week, we have done so in this book. Traditional names refer to pagan gods, for example sun-day and moon-day. Tiu was a supposed god of the sky. Wednesday is Oden's day, followed by Thor's day. Frig or Freyja in Friday refers to Odin's wife, and Saturday refers to Saturn. Therefore most of the days are simply numbered in this book, reserving honor for God alone.

Origin & Purpose:

The translator and editor of this volume created it in order to aid his own hourly prayer with the ultimate desire to pray without ceasing. The four oldest Christian traditions (Roman Catholicism, Eastern Orthodoxy, Oriental Orthodoxy, and the Assyrian Church of the East) all use books of prayer throughout the day, books which consist primarily of prayers written outside of Scripture. Since most Protestants lack such a time tested aid, the translator first edited the King James Version of the Psalms into hourly segments and published it under the title of "The Weekly Psalter," with sixteen hourly readings per day for seven days.

In practice, however, the Psalms too often reflected decidedly non-Christian requests for revenge on human enemies. Many of the Psalmist's prayers for revenge can be redirected toward our spiritual enemies, but not all. For example, the Psalmist at one point prays that the mother of his enemy would not be forgiven. This volume omits some of the most vengeful verses. Also omitted here are many passages of the Psalms which sing *about* God, rather than singing or praying directly *to* God. This volume replenishes those passages with other prayers of Scripture primarily from the New Testament for an average six minutes of prayer per hour, a tithe of each hour. There are also four "Night Watches" comprised of the longest Psalms, to aid evening and nighttime vigils of prayer. Two additional segments complete this volume; one at the start of the book contains passages about putting on "the new man," and one at the close of this book contains passages related to communion in our Lord's body and blood.

Let us prayerfully agree that Jesus of Nazareth is the Psalm 2 "Anointed," which is *Messiah* in Hebrew and *Christ* in Greek. He is the King of kings and the Master of masters who reigns now in the hearts of His peaceful slaves. To his name we give glory, honor, and obedience now and forever. Truly, He is Lord!

In the two thousand twenty third
year of our Anointed Lord Jesus,
Matthew Bryan

Putting on the New Creation

As many as were baptized into Anointed King Jesus, we were baptized into his death.

Therefore we were buried together with him through baptism into death; so that just as the Anointed King was roused from the dead ones through the Father's glory, in this way we too should walk in novelty of life.

For if we have become planted together in the likeness of his death, yet also will we be of the resurrection,

Knowing that our old person was co-crucified, so that the body of sin would be shut down, for us to no longer be enslaved to sin;

For the one having died has been rendered righteous, away from sin.

Yet if we died together with the Anointed King, we trust that we will also live together with him.

In this way, count yourselves to be dead to sin yet living to God in Anointed King Jesus our Master!

Present yourselves to God as those who are living from the dead, and present your organs to God as weapons of righteousness![2]

For whom he knew in advance, he also marked

out in advance to be conformed of the image of his Son, for him to be the Firstborn among many siblings[3]

Clothe yourselves in the Master, Anointed King Jesus[4]

Even as truth is in Jesus, if indeed you heard and were taught in him,

For you to put away the old human who is according to the former behavior, being corroded according to the lusts of delusion,

To be renewed in the spirit of your mind

And to put on the new human who is according to God, created in righteousness and holiness of the Truth.[5]

Slip on God's full armor, for you to be able to stand before the ambushes of the slanderous one;

For to us, the wrestling is not toward blood and flesh but toward the rulers, toward the authorities, toward the world powers of the darkness of this age, toward the spiritual things of wickedness among the heavenly realms.

Therefore take up the full armor of God, in order that you would be able to stand opposed in the evil day, and to stand as overpowering all things.

Therefore stand, belting your loins in truth and slipping on the breastplate of righteousness

And binding your feet in the preparation of the gospel of peace,

Against all things, lifting the shield of trust by which you will be able to extinguish all the missiles which have been enflamed from the evil one;

Receive also the helmet of liberation and the sword of the Spirit, which is the utterance of God,

Praying in the Spirit through every prayer and plea in every season, and remaining awake for this same reason in all perseverance and pleading about all the saints[6]

If someone is in Anointed King Jesus, there is a new creation. the old things passed away; behold, all things have become new![7]

Therefore if you were roused together with the Anointed King, seek the things above, where the Anointed King is continually sitting at God's right hand.

Contemplate the things above, not the things upon the earth.

For you died, and your life has been concealed together with the Anointed King in God.

Whenever the Anointed King who is your life should become visible, then you also will become visible in glory.

Therefore mortify your organs which are upon the earth, fornication, uncleanness, lust, evil desire, and greed which is idolatry,

On account of which things, God's anger comes upon the children of stubbornness,

In which things you formerly walked when you were living in them;

Yet now you too, bury away all those things, passion, anger, evil, calumniation, and shameful speech from your mouth!

Do not falsify to one another, stripping off the old human with his practices

And slipping on the new human, the one being renewed into a recognition which is according to the image of the one creating him[8]

Viewing the glory of the Lord as in a mirror, we all with unveiled face are being transformed into the same image from glory into glory, even as being from the Lord, the Spirit.[9]

1st Watch of Night

Therefore watch, for you known not what hour the master of the house comes, at evening, or midnight, or cock's crow, or dawn.[10]

Our Father in heaven, your name be hallowed,

Your kingdom come, and your will happen on earth as it does in heaven,

Give us today our daily bread,

And release for us our debts, as we ourselves also release our debtors;

And bring us not into testing, but rush us away from the evil one. for yours is the kingdom and the power and the glory into the ages; amen![11]

In my whole heart I will sing praise to you,
O LORD, I will recount all your marvelous deeds!

I will make merry and leap joyfully in you, I will strum to your name, O most High;

When my enemies are turned away backwards, they will weaken and perish away from your sight,

For you accomplished my judgment and my justice; you sat upon the throne, judging righteousness.

You destroyed the irreverent person, and you

rebuked nations; you blotted out their name into the coming age and into age of age;

The enemy's swords completely failed, and you dismantled the cities; their memory perished with a roar.

And the LORD remains into the coming age, he prepared his throne in judgment,

And he will judge the inhabited world in righteousness, he will judge the peoples in uprightness.

The LORD became a refuge for the needy one, a rescuer in affliction at the right times;

And those who know your name must expect upon you, O LORD, for you did not forsake those who seek after you.

Strum to the LORD who dwells in Zion, announce among the nations his practices,

For he, observing the bloodshed, was mindful of them; he did not forget the outcry of the needy.

Rescue me, O LORD, behold my humiliation from my enemies, you who lift me out from the gates of death,

So that I would proclaim all your praises in the gates of the daughter of Zion; I will leap for joy at your liberation!

Arise, O LORD, let a human not prevail, let the

nations be judged before you;

Establish a lawgiver over them, O LORD, let the nations know that they are but humans.

Interlude.

Why have you departed afar, O LORD? why do you overlook at opportune times during affliction?

When the irreverent person gloats, the poor one is scorched; they are seized by the debates which they argue.

For the sinful person praises himself amid the passions of his soul, and the one who does injustice blesses himself within;

The sinful man provoked the Lord, saying: According to the length of his anger, he will not seek me out. God is not in in his sight.

His ways are defiled in every season, your judgments are canceled from before his face; he takes dominion over all his enemies.

He said in his heart, I could not be shaken, I will not be in adversity from generation into generation.

His mouth is full of cursing and bitterness and deceit, under his tongue are toil and trouble.

He lurks in ambush with the wealthy in the secret places, to slay an innocent one; his eyes stare into the needy person;

He lays wait in secret like a lion in his burrow; he lays wait to snatch a poor person, to snatch a poor man when drawing him away;

In his trap he will humiliate him; yet he will stoop and fall while he is overpowering the needy ones.

He said in his heart, God has forgotten and hid his face entirely from seeing.

Arise, LORD God, uplift your hand, do not forget the needy ones!

Why did the irreverent one provoke God? for he said in his heart: He will not seek out.

You saw; for you observe pain and sorrow in order to deliver them into your hand; therefore the poor one has been abandoned to you; you yourself were the rescuer to the orphan.

O break the arm of the sinful and wicked one! his sin will be investigated; and because of it, he could not be found.

The LORD will reign into the coming age and into age of age; O nations, you will perish from his land.

The LORD heard the desire of the humble; the readiness of their heart attaches to your ear,

To judge for the orphan and the lowly one, so that no human should continue to boast upon the earth.[12]

O God, my God, attend unto me; why did you abandon me? The accounts of my transgressions are far from my liberation.

O my God, I will cry out in the daytime, and you will not listen; even in the night, and not for my thoughtlessness.

Yet you, the praise of Israel, dwell among the holy ones.

Our fathers hoped upon you; they hoped, and you delivered them.

They cried out to you and were liberated; they hoped upon you and were not turned away.

I, however, am a worm and not human, a derision of humanity and a scorn of people.

All who observe me sneer at me, they shook their head, and they said with the lips:

He hoped upon the LORD; let him rescue him; he must liberate him, because he wants him.

For you are the one who drew me out of the belly, you were my hope from the breasts of my mother.

Unto you I was flung from the womb; from my mother's belly, you are my God.

Do not depart from me; for trouble is near, for there is no one else to give me aid.

Many are the calves who encircled me, stout bulls surrounded me;

They opened their mouth at me like a lion snapping and roaring.

I was poured out like water, and all my bones were spread out; my heart became like melted wax in the midst of my stomach;

My strength was dried out like pottery, and my tongue has been glued to my throat; and you brought me down into the dust of death.

For many dogs encircled me, an evildoing crowd surrounded me; they gouged my hands and my feet.

I counted out all my bones; they pondered deeply and looked upon me.

They distributed my garments among them and cast lots for my clothing.

Yet you, O LORD, delay not my rescue! give heed to assisting me!

Deliver my soul from the sword, and my only begotten from the hand of a dog.

Liberate me from the lion's mouth, and my lowliness from the horns of one-horned beasts.

I will recount your name to my siblings; I will sing hymns to you in the midst of a congregation.

Those who fear the LORD, praise him; all ye seed of Jacob, glorify him; let all the seed of Israel fear him!

For he did not despise nor abhor the pleading of the poor, neither did he turn his face away from me; and when I had cried out for him, he listened closely to me.

From you is my praise in the great congregation; I will repay my vows in front of those who fear him

The needy shall eat and be filled, and those who seek after him shall praise the LORD; their hearts will live unto age of age.

All the ends of the earth will be mindful and turn back toward the LORD, and all the families of the nations will bow down before you,

For the kingdom is of the LORD, and he himself overrules the nations.

The stout ones of the earth ate and bowed down; all those who descend into the earth will fall down before him. and my soul lives for him.

My seed will slave unto him; the coming generation will be announced to the Master.

They will announce his righteousness to a people which shall be born, because the Lord performed it.[13]

Listen closely to my prayer, O LORD, and let my cry come before you.

You would not turn your face away from me;

incline your ear toward me in the day when I am afflicted; quickly hear from me in the day when I call upon you!

For my days went up like smoke, and my bones burned together like firewood.

My heart was struck and withered away like grass, so that I forgot to eat of my bread.

My bones cleaved to my flesh from the sound of my groaning.

I was made like a pelican in a wasteland, I became like a long eared owl in a building.

I did not sleep, and I became like a sparrow isolating on a roof.

The whole day my enemies were reviling me, and those who praise me were swearing against me.

For I ate soot like bread, and I mixed my drink with sobbing

From the face of your anger and your passion; for you were uplifting me, and you broke me down.

My days were slanted like a shadow, and I withered away like the grass.

Yet you, O LORD, you remain into the coming age, and the awareness of you continues into generation and generation.

Rising up, you will pity Zion, for it is the season

to pity her, for the season approaches;

For your slaves were pleased with her stones,
and they will take pity on her dust.

And the nations will fear the name of the LORD,
and all the kings of the land will fear your glory,

For the LORD will build up Zion and appear in
his glory!

He observed the prayer of the humble and did
not despise their pleading.

Let this prayer be inscribed for a different
generation; and the people being created shall
praise the LORD,

For he peered out from his holy height, the
LORD looked out of heaven upon the land

To hear the groaning of those who were
bound, to release the children of those who
were put to death,

To announce the name of the LORD in Zion, and
his praise in Jerusalem

When the peoples and kings are gathered
together to serve unto the LORD.

From the beginning, O LORD, you founded the
land; and the skies are the works of your hands.

They will perish, yet you will remain, and they
will all age away like a garment. you change
them like a cloak, and they shall be changed;

Yet you yourself are the same, and your years

will not be exhausted.

The children of your slaves will encamp, and their seed will be prospered into the coming age.[14]

Confess unto the LORD, for he is kind, for into the coming age is his deliverance;

Confess unto the God of gods, for into the coming age is his deliverance;

Confess unto the Master of masters, for into the coming age is his deliverance;

To the one who alone makes great wonders, for into the coming age is his deliverance;

To the one making the heavens in understanding, for into the coming age is his deliverance;

To the one stabilizing the land upon the waters, for into the coming age is his deliverance;

To the one alone making the great lights, for into the coming age is his deliverance,

The sun as the day's authority, for into the coming age is his deliverance,

The moon and stars as the night's authority, for into the coming age is his deliverance;

To the one who strikes Egypt with their firstborn, for into the coming age is his deliverance,

And leads Israel out of their midst, for into the coming age is his deliverance,

By a mighty hand and by a lofty arm, for into the coming age is his deliverance;

To the one who divides the red sea into parts, for into the coming age is his deliverance,

And leads Israel through its midst, for into the coming age is his deliverance,

And scatters Pharaoh and his strength into the red sea, for into the coming age is his deliverance;

To the one who leads his people through the wilderness, for into the coming age is his deliverance; to the one who brings water out of a sharp rock, for into the coming age is his deliverance;

To the one who strikes great kings, for into the coming age is his deliverance,

And slays mighty kings, for into the coming age is his deliverance,

Sihon king of the Amorites, for into the coming age is his deliverance,

And Og the king of Bashan, for into the coming age is his deliverance,

And he gave their land as an inheritance, for into the coming age is his deliverance,

A heritage for Israel his slave, for into the

coming age is his deliverance.

Because the Lord remembered us in our lowliness, for into the coming age is his deliverance,

And he ransomed us from our enemies, for into the coming age is his deliverance;

He who gives nourishment to all flesh, for into the coming age is his deliverance.

Confess unto the God of heaven, for into the coming age is his deliverance; confess unto the Master of masters, for into the coming age is his deliverance.[15]

2nd Watch of Night

Blessed are those slaves whom the master would find watching when he comes. firmly I say to you that he will gird himself and will recline them. and coming, he will serve them.

If he would come in the second watch, and would come in the third watch, and would find them this way, blessed are those slaves.[16]

Our Father in heaven, your name be hallowed,

Your kingdom come, and your will become on earth as it is in heaven,

Give us today our daily bread,

And release for us our debts, as we ourselves also release our debtors;

And bring us not into testing, but rush us away from the evil one. for yours is the kingdom and the power and the glory into the ages; amen![17]

O LORD, my strength, I shall love you.

The LORD is my stability and my refuge and my rescuer; my God is my deliverer, and I will hope upon him, my overshielder and the horn of my liberation, my helper!

Praising, I will call upon the LORD; and I will be liberated from my enemies.

The pains of death surrounded me, and the

rivers of the lawless ones troubled me.

The pains of hades encircled me; the traps of death went before me.

When they were afflicting me, I called upon the LORD and I cried out unto my God; he heard my voice from his holy temple, and my cry entered before him into his ears.

Then the land became shaken and trembling, and the foundations of the hills were agitated and shook, because God was angered.

Smoke ascended in his anger, and fire from his face was lit aflame; coals were kindled from it.

And he bent the sky and descended, and darkness was under his feet.

He mounted upon cherubim and flew, he flew upon the wings of the wind.

He set darkness as his hiding place; round about him was his tent, dark water in clouds of mists.

From the brightness before him, the clouds passed through; there was hail and coals of fire.

The LORD thundered out of heaven, and the most High gave his voice;

And he sent out arrows and scattered them; and he multiplied lightnings and stirred them up.

The fountains of the waters appeared, and the

foundations of the inhabited world were uncovered from your rebuke, O Lord, from the breathing of the breath of your wrath.

He sent from above and took me, he accepted me out of many waters.

He rushed me out from my strong enemies and from those who hate me, for they were stationed over me.

They went before me in the day of my mistreatment, and the Lord became my support

And led me out into the open; he will deliver me, for he desires me. He will rush me out from my powerful enemies and from those who hate me.

And the Lord will reward me according to my righteousness, and he will reward me according to the purity of my hands,

For I have guarded the paths of the Lord and did not break devotion from my God,

For all his judgments were before me, and I did not withdraw his statutes from me.

And I will be spotless with him, and I will guard myself away from my lawlessness.

And the Lord will reward me according to my righteousness and according to the purity of my hands before his eyes.

You will be hallowed with a holy person, and
you will be guiltless with a guiltless man,

And with the preferred person you will be
preferred, and with a twisted one you will twist
about.

For you will liberate your lowly people, and you
will lower the eyes of the lofty ones.

For you O LORD, will illuminate my lamp; O my
God, you will illuminate my darkness.

For by you, I will be rushed away from a gang;
and by my God, I will overstep a barricade.

As for my God, his path is without blemish, the
words of the LORD have been smelted, he is the
overshielder of all those who expect upon him.

For who is a god except the LORD? and who is a
god except our God?

God is the one who girds me about with power,
and he set my path without a blemish,

He who repairs my feet like those of a deer,
and stands me up upon the heights;

Instructing my hands for war, you set my arms
like a bronze bow;

And you gave to me a shield of liberation, and
your right hand assisted me, and your
discipline straightened me toward the goal,
and your discipline itself will instruct me.

You broadened my tracks beneath me, and my

steps did not weaken.

I will pursue my enemies and overtake them, and I will not turn away until they would faint;

I will afflict them, and they cannot stand, they will fall beneath my feet.

For you girded me about with strength for the battle; you shackled beneath me the feet of all who arise against me

And you gave the back of my enemies to me, and you destroyed those who hate me.

They screamed, and there was no one to make them safe; even to the LORD but he hearkened not to them.

I ground them like the dust against the wind, I will grind them like the mire of streets.

You will rush me out of the controversies of the people, and you will establish me for the head of nations; a people served me whom I did not know,

At the hearing of the ear, they obeyed me; yet strange sons lied to me,

The strange sons became old and wavered away from their paths.

The LORD lives, and blessed be my God! let the God of my liberation be exalted,

The God who gives vengeance to me and who subdues peoples underneath me,

The one who rushes me out from my wrathful enemies; you will elevate me from those who arise against me, you will rush me away from an unjust man.

Therefore I will acknowledge you among the nations, O LORD, and strum unto your name,

The one who magnifies the liberation of his king and makes a rescue for his anointed, for David and for his seed until the coming age![18]

O God, we heard in our ears. our fathers reported to us the work which you worked in their days, the days of old.

Your hand obliterated the nations, and you planted them; you injured peoples and cast them out.

For they did not inherit the land by their sword, and their arm did not liberate them; but your right hand and your arm performed it, even the light of your countenance, because you took pleasure in them.

You are my King and my God, the one who commands the deliverances of Jacob.

In you we will gore our enemies, and in your name we will disdain those who rise up against us;

For I will not hope upon my bow, and my

sword will not save me;

Because you liberated us from those who afflict us, and you shamed those who hate us.

In God we will be commended the whole day, and in your name will we give thanks into the age to come.

Interlude.

Yet now you drove us away and shamed us and will not go out among our forces;

You turned us backwards from our enemies, and the ones who hate us were seizing plunders for themselves.

You gave us as sheep for meat and scattered us among the nations;

You gave up your people without a price, and there was no amount in their exchange.

You put us as a derision for our neighbors, a scorn and a mockery to those round about us.

You put us as an example among the nations, a shaking of the head among the peoples.

My embarrassment is before me the whole day, and the shame of my face has covered me

From the voice of an insulting and babbling person, from the face of a hostile and persecuting person.

These things all came upon us, and we did not forget you, and we did not act unjustly with your covenant,

And our heart did not depart into the things behind; and you did not turn our footsteps away from your path.

For you humbled us in a place of suffering, and a shadow of death covered us.

If we forgot the name of our God and if we spread out our hands to a different god,

Will God not search out these things? for he knows the hidden things of the heart.

For we are put to death the whole day for your sake; we are accounted as sheep of slaughter.

Be awakened, O Lord! why do you sleep? arise, do not completely drive us away.

Why does your face turn away, and why do you forget our poverty and our affliction?

For our soul was humbled into the dust; our belly was joined into the ground.

Arise, O Lord, give us aid, and ransom us for your name's sake![19]

Into the coming age O LORD, I will sing of your lovingkindnesses; into generation and generation I will report your truth with my mouth,

For you said, Into the coming age, lovingkindness shall be built up. your truth will be prepared in the heavens.

I covenanted a covenant with my select ones, I swore unto David my slave:

I will prepare your seed until the coming age, and I will build up your throne into generation and generation.

Interlude.

O Lord, the heavens will confess your marvels, and your truth in the congregation of holy ones.

For among the clouds, who will be equaled unto the Lord, who among the sons of God will be made like unto the Lord?

Being glorified in the council of the holy ones, he is God, great and formidable before all those round about him.

O Lord God of armies, who is like unto you? O Lord, powerful are you and your truth surrounding you.

You overrule the might of the sea, and you pacify the tossing of its waves.

You humbled the arrogant one like a wounded man, and you dispersed your enemies by the arm of your power.

The skies are yours, and the land is yours; you founded the inhabitation and its fullness.

You created the north and the seas; Mount

Tabor and Hermon will leap joyfully in your name.

Yours is the arm with dominion; let your hand be empowered! your right hand be uplifted!

Righteousness and judgment are the readiness of your throne, lovingkindness and truth will go before your face.

Blessed is the people that knows a joyful noise; O LORD, they will proceed in the light of your countenance,

And in your name they will leap joyfully all day, and in your righteousness they shall be uplifted.

For you yourself are the boast of their strength, and our horn will be uplifted in your goodwill.

For assistance is of the LORD and of the Holy One of Israel, our King.

Then you spoke to your holy ones in a vision and said: I appointed aid for a mighty one, I exalted a favorite one out of my people;

I found David my slave; I anointed him in my holy oil.

For my hand will assist him, and my arm will make him strong;

An enemy will not profit by him, and a son of lawlessness will not put forth a hand to harm him;

And I will beat down his foes from before his face and turn away those who hate him.

And my truth and my lovingkindness will be with him, and his horn will be elevated in my name;

And I will set his hand in a sea, and his right hand amid the rivers.

He will invoke me, saying: You are my father, my God, and the helper of my salvation;

And I will place him as firstborn, lofty amid the presence of the kings of the land.

Into the coming age I will guard my lovingkindness for him, and my covenant will be faithful unto him;

And I will place his seed into age of age, and his throne like the days of heaven.

And if his children should abandon my law and proceed not in my judgments,

And if they should tread upon my statutes and guard not my commandments,

Then I will visit their violations with a rod, and their sins with a whip,

Yet I would not disperse my lovingkindness away from him, nor enact an injustice with my truth,

Nor shall I tread upon my covenant, and I would not displace that which proceeds through my lips.

Once did I swear by my holiness: Unto David I shall not lie,

His seed will remain into the coming age, and his throne will be before me like the sun,

And like the moon having been made firm into the coming age; and trustworthy is the testimony in heaven.

Interlude.

Yet you pushed away and despised, you cast off your anointed;

You overturned the covenant of your slave, you trod his sanctuary into the ground.

You elevated the right hand of his enemies, you made all his enemies rejoice;

You turned away your aid from his sword and did not assist him in the battle.

How long, O LORD, will you turn away completely, and your anger be inflamed like fire?

Remember what my substance is; did you create all the children of men in vain?

Who is a man who will live and not see death? will he rescue his soul from the hand of hades?

Interlude.

Where are your lovingkindnesses of old, O

LORD, which you swore to David in your truth?

Be mindful O LORD, of the reviling of your slaves, which I upheld in my bosom from many nations,

With which your enemies reviled, O LORD, with which they reviled the change of your anointed.

O blessed be the LORD into the age to come! amen, amen![20]

3rd Watch of Night

At midnight I was awakened to confess to you about the judgments of your righteousness.

Alef

All blessed are those who are without blemish in the path, those who proceed in the law of the LORD.

All blessed are those who search after his testimonies; they will wholeheartedly seek after him.

For those who work lawlessness do not walk in his paths.

You have commanded for your laws to be guarded well.

O that my paths would be kept straight, in order to guard your statutes.

Then I would not be ashamed when I look attentively at all your commands.

When I have learned your judgments of righteousness, O Lord, I will acknowledge you with uprightness of heart.

I will guard your statutes; do not vehemently

forsake me.

Bet

By what shall a youth make straight his path?
by guarding your words.

In my whole heart I sought after you; thrust me
not away from your commandment.

I hid your oracles in my heart, so that I would
never sin against you.

Blessed are you, O LORD; teach me your
statutes.

By my lips I declared all the judgments of your
mouth.

I delighted in the path of your testimonies, as I
would delight in all wealth.

I will meditate in your commandments and
ponder your pathways.

I will train in your statutes, I will not neglect
your words.

Gimel

Give recompense to your slave; I will live and
guard your words.

Uncover my eyes, and I will consider your
wonders from your law.

I am alien to this land; do not hide your
commandments from me.

In every season my soul longed to desire your decrees.

You rebuked those who esteem themselves; those who bend away from your commandments are cursed.

Take away from me insults and belittlements, for I sought out your testimonies.

For the rulers sat and railed against me, yet your slave meditated in your statutes.

For your testimonies are my concern, and your statutes are my counselors.

Dalet

Down to dust did my soul adhere; O vivify me according to your word!

I described my paths, and you heard from me; teach me your decrees.

Make me to comprehend the path of your decrees, and I will meditate in your wonders.

My soul droops from disregard; stabilize me in your declarations!

Detach from me the path of unrighteousness, and deliver me by your law.

The path of truth I chose, I forgot not your judgments.

I was adjoined to your testimonies; O LORD, do not put me to shame.

3rd Watch of Night

I ran the path of your commandments, when
you opened wide my heart.

Hey

Help me receive the law, O LORD, the path of
your statutes; and through everything I will
hunt for it.

Help me to comprehend, and I will hunt out
your law and guard it in my whole heart.

Guide me in the path of your commandments,
for I have desired it.

Bend my heart into your testimonies and not
into holding possessions.

Divert my eyes from beholding futilities;
enliven me in your path!

Establish your utterance in your slave in order
to fear you.

Lift away from me the reproach which I had
imagined, for your judgments are kind.

Behold, I yearned for your commandments;
vivify me in your righteousness!

Vav

Verge your aid and salvation toward me,
O LORD, according to your revelation.

And I will respond with a reason to those who
vilify me, for I have hoped upon your words.

And do not remove the word of truth completely from my mouth; for I placed hope upon your judgments.

And I will guard your law through everything, for the coming age and into age of age.

I was traveling in spaciousness, because I sought out your directives.

And I was speaking within your testimonies before kings, and I did not turn away in shame.

And I was meditating in your commandments, which I vehemently loved.

And I elevated my hands toward your commandments, which I loved, and I was contemplating in your statutes.

Zayin

Zip in mind within your slave your word which gave me hope.

It encouraged me in my humbling, for your word vivified me.

The arrogant transgressed the law entirely, yet I did not lean away from your law.

From of old, O LORD, I was made mindful of your judgments and was encouraged.

Despair siezed me because of sinful ones, those who abandon your law.

Musical were your statutes to me in the land of

my sojourning.

Mindful was I of your name in the night, and I guarded your law, O Lord.

This happened within me, because I sought out your statutes.

Het

How you are my portion, Lord! I affirmed that I would guard your law.

Whole heartedly I implored of your presence: Help me according to your utterance!

I reckoned your paths and turned back my feet into your testimonies.

I was prepared to guard your commands, and I was not disturbed.

The cords of sinful ones were entwined around me, and I did not forget your law.

At midnight I was awakened to confess to you about the judgments of your righteousness.

I am a companion of all who fear you and of those who guard your commandments.

The earth is heaped full of your aid, O Lord; teach unto me your statutes.

Tet

Tenderness you performed with your slave, O Lord, according unto your word.

Teach me tenderness and correction and knowledge, for I hoped upon your commandments.

I caused disharmony before I was humbled; because of this I guarded your utterance.

Tender are you, O Lord; and in your tenderness you taught me your statutes.

To me the injustice of the arrogant was multiplied, yet I will search out your commandments with my whole heart.

Their heart was curdled like milk; yet as for me, I contemplated your law.

'Tis good for me that you humbled me, so that I would train in your statutes.

To me the law from your mouth is good, above thousands of coins of gold and silver.

<u>Yod</u>

Your hands made me and sculpted me; make me to understand, and I will learn your commandments.

Those who fear you will observe me and be glad, for in your words I put expectation.

I knew that your judgments are righteous, O Lord, and you humbled me in truth.

Let your lovingkindness indeed come to pass, to encourage me according to your utterance to your slave.

Let your compassions come to me, and I will live; for your law is my concern.

Let the arroganet be turned back in shame, for they transgressed unjustly toward me; yet will I meditate in your commandments.

Let those who fear you return to me, and those who know your testimonies.

My heart must become blameless in your statutes, so that I would never be turned back in shame.

Kaph

Continually my soul faints for your liberation, and I expected in your word.

My eyes keep fainting for your utterance and saying, When will you comfort me?

For I became like a wineskin in frost; yet your statutes I did not forget.

How many are the days of your slave? when will you make a judgment for me from those who persecute me?

Transgressors recounted speculations to me, but not like your law, O Lord.

All your commandments are truth. they persecute me unjustly; rescue me!

They almost finished me in the ground; yet

your commands I did not abandon.

According to your lovingkindness, enliven me! and I will keep watch over the testimonies from your mouth.

Lamed

Lasting in heaven, O LORD, is your word into the age to come.

Into generation and generation is your truth; you laid the land as a foundation, and it lasts.

The day lasts in your arrangement, because all things are your slaves.

In my lowliness I would be lost, if your law were not my meditation.

Into the coming age I could not overlook your rules, for by them you livened me, O Lord.

Yours am I, liberate me! for I sought out your rules.

Sinful ones lurked for me to destroy me; your testimonies I contemplated.

The limit of all perfection I saw; your commandment is wonderfully broad.

Mem

Much did I love your law, O Lord; it is my meditation the whole day.

More than my enemies, you made me wise

according to your commandment, for it is mine into the age to come.

I comprehended above those who teach me, for your testimonies are my meditation.

More than the elders, I comprehended, for I sought out your commandments.

My feet did I block from every evil path, so that I might guard your words.

I leaned not away from your decrees, for you framed laws for me.

More than honey and honeycomb in my mouth, how sweet are your statements in my throat!

I comprehended from your commands; so I held malice toward every path of mischief, because you framed laws for me.

Nun

Unto my feet your word is a lantern, and light unto my trails.

I stood and have covenanted to guard the judgments of your righteousness.

Intensely I was humbled, O LORD; enliven me according to your word.

Usher in the freewill offerings of my mouth, O LORD, and instruct unto me your ordinances.

Continually my soul was in my hands, and I

neglected not your law;

Sinners installed a snare for me, and I turned not astray from your commandments.

I inherited your testimonies unendingly, for they are the rejoicing of my heart.

I inclined my heart to always practice your ordinances on account of their reward.

Samekh

Seethed did I against the lawless, and loved did I your law.

You are my savior and my support; I set expectation into your word.

Split from me, ye evildoers, for I will seek out the commandments of my God.

Support me according to your statement, and I shall live; you would not shame me away from my expectation.

Assist me, and I will be saved, and unceasingly I will study your statutes.

You despised all who apostasized from your statutes, for their sentiment is unjust.

All the sinful ones of the land I accounted as transgressing, therefore I consistently loved your testimonies.

Spike my flesh with the fear of you, for I was scared by your decisions.

Ayin

I accomplished judgment and righteousness; do not deliver me to those who harm me.

Accept your slave into good, let not the arrogant incriminate me.

My eyes faint away for your liberation and for the utterance of your righteousness.

Do with your slave according to your compassion, and instruct unto me your statutes.

Your slave am I; educate me, and I will know your testimonies.

It is time for the LORD to act; they have scattered your law.

On account of this, I loved your edicts far above gold and topaz.

On account of this, I kept straightforth toward all your edicts; I hated every unjust path.

Peh

Ponderous are your testimonies, therefore my soul pursued them.

The pointing out of your words will enlighten and instruct infants.

I parted my mouth and drew breath, because I pined for your precepts.

Peer upon me and preserve me according to

the judgment of those who love your name.

Straighten my steps according to your pronouncement; and let not all lawlessness overpower me.

Ransom me from people's extortion; and will I guard your precepts.

Make your face apparent before your slave, and teach me your statutes.

My eyes plunged like rivers of waters, for they did not guard your law.

Tsade

Testified as righteous are you, O LORD; and your judgment is upright.

Intensely you commanded your testimonies as righteousness and truth.

The fervor of your house torched me, for my enemies neglected your words.

Intensely refined is your utterance, and your slave has loved it.

I am younger and being disregarded; I did not forget your statutes.

Your righteousness is righteousness into the age to come, and your law is the truth.

Tribulation and compulsion found me; your commandments are my concern.

Your testimonies are righteousness into the

coming age; cause me to fathom them, and I shall live.

Qof

Called out did I with my whole heart; hear me, O LORD; I will seek out your decrees.

I cried out to you: Liberate me, and I will keep watch over your testimonies!

In the dead of night I anticipated and cried out; I expected in your words.

My eyes ran forth before sunrise, to contemplate your utterances.

According to your compassion, O LORD, hear from my voice; vivify me according to your judgment!

Those who persecute me brought anarchy to me; they were displaced from your law.

Near are you, O LORD; and all your commandments are truth.

Anciently I knew from your testimonies, for you laid them as a foundation into the coming age.

Resh

Regard my humiliation and remove me, for I did not overlook your law.

Judge my judgment, and ransom me; vivify me because of your word!

Safety is far away from sinful ones, for they did not pursue your ordinances.

Your compassions are many, O Lord; enliven me according to your judgments!

Many are those who persecute me and oppress me; I did not reverse from your testimonies.

I regarded those who were breaking covenant, and I was wasting away; for they did not guard your utterances.

Behold that I loved your commands; O Lord, vivify me in your lovingkindness!

The origin of your words is truth, and into the coming age are the judgments of your righteousness.

Shin

Shamelessly did the rulers persecute me, and my heart was frightened of your words.

I will exult at your statements like the one who finds many spoils.

I hated and shunned injustice, yet I have loved your law.

At the judgments of your righteousness, I praised you seven times a day.

There is much peace in those who love your law, and in them there is not a snare.

I was anticipating your liberation, O Lord; and I

loved your commandments.

My soul guarded your testimonies, and I loved them surpassingly.

I guarded your commandments and your testimonies, for all my paths are before you, O Lord.

<u>Tav</u>

To your presence, LORD, let my pleading approach; cause me to understand according to your utterance.

Let my petition enter in front of you; rescue me according unto your utterance!

An ode poured forth from my lips whenever you would teach me your statutes.

My tongue will speak your utterance, for all your edicts are righteousness.

Let your hand happen to liberate me, because I preferred your commandments.

I longed for your liberty, O LORD; and your law is my meditation.

My soul will live and praise you; and your judgments shall assist me.

I was strayed like a sheep having been lost; seek out your slave, for I did not forget your commandments.[21]

4th Watch of Night

My eyes ran forth before sunrise, to contemplate your utterances.

In the fourth watch of the night, Jesus came toward them, walking upon the sea.[22]

Save me, O God; for the waters came in as far as my soul.

I was stuck into the mud of the deep, and there is no support; I came into the depths of the sea, and a windstorm plunged me down.

I wearied of screaming, my throat chafed, my eyes fainted from expecting upon my God.

They who hate me for naught were multiplied more than the hairs of my head, my enemies were empowered who unjustly persecute me; then I was repaying things which I did not seize.

O God, you knew my senselessness, and my discordant deeds were not hidden from you.

Let those who await you turn not away from me in shame, O LORD God of armies! let those who seek you be not embarrassed at me, O

God of Israel,

Because for your sake I bore reproach; embarrassment covered my face.

I became estranged to my siblings, and an foreigner to my mother's children,

For the fervor of your house melted me; and upon me fell the reproaches of those who reproach you.

I bent my soul in fasting, and it became a reproach toward me;

Even my clothing became sackcloth, and I became a proverb to them.

They who sit in the gate chattered against me, and those who drink wine strummed songs about me.

Yet I said in my prayer to you, O LORD, The season of goodwill, O God, is in the vastness of your lovingkindness; O hear from me in the truth of your liberation!

Liberate me from the mud, so that I would not be implanted; O that I would be rushed away from those who hate me, and out of the deep of the waters;

Let the windstorm of waters not plunge me down, nor the deep gulp me down, nor the pit enclose its mouth over me.

Listen to me, O LORD, for your lovingkindness is

practical; look upon me according to the magnitude of your pity.

You would not turn your face away from your servant; hearken to me swiftly, for I am afflicted!

Take heed to my soul and ransom it; rescue me for the sake of my enemies.

You know my insult and my rejection and embarrassment; all those who afflict me are before you.

My soul anticipated the reviling and heaviness; and I awaited a sympathizing one, and he did not exist—and for encouragers, and I did not find them.

They gave gall for my food, and they gave me vinegar for my thirst.

Let their table before them become a trap and a recompense and a snare!

Let their eyes be darkened to see not! bend their back continually!

Pour out your anger on them, and may the passion of your anger take hold of them.

Let their homestead become deserted, and let there be no one who dwells among their tents;

For they persecuted the one whom you struck, and they added to the pain of your wounds.

Poor and pained am I, O God, and the salvation

of your countenance assisted me.

I will praise the name of God with a song, and I will magnify him in praise,

And it will please the Lord more than a young calf bearing horns and hoofs.

O let the poor behold and make merry; seek ye after God! even your soul must seek after him,

For the Lord heard from the poor, and he did not despise those who have been shackled.

Let the skies and the land praise him, the sea and all things creeping in them!

For God will liberate Zion, and the cities of Judah shall be built up, and they will dwell there and inherit her;

And the seed of his slaves will occupy her, and those who love his name will encamp within her.[23]

The God of vengeance is the Lord. the God of vengeance spoke boldly.

You who judge the earth, be lifted high! repay a reward to the arrogant.

O Lord, how long will the sinful ones, how long will the sinful ones boast?

Will they declare and speak injustice? will all those who work lawlessness speak it?

Lord, they humiliated your people and harmed

your inheritance.

They slew the widow and immigrant, and they murdered orphans.

They even said, The LORD will not observe, nor will the God of Jacob comprehend.

Comprehend indeed, O thoughtless ones among the people! and ye dull ones, think one time.

Does the one implanting the ear not hear? does the one forming the eye not consider?

Will the one who instructs the nations, he who teaches a human knowledge, not rebuke?

The LORD knows the disputes of people, that they are useless.

Blessed is the person whom you, O LORD, would train and teach him from your law,

To calm him from the evil days, until a pit was dug for the sinner.

For the LORD will not drive away his people, nor will he forsake his inheritance

Until righteousness will return for judgment, and all the upright in heart will hold it.

Interlude.

Who will stand up for me against evildoers? or who will stand beside me against the workers of lawlessness?

Unless the Lord rescued me, my soul soon would have sojourned in hades.

If I was saying, My foot has been shaken, then your lovingkindness rescues me, O Lord;

According to the multitude of my pains in my heart, so much did your encouragements love my soul.

Will a throne of lawlessness be present before you, which forms trouble toward an ordinance?

They will hunt after the soul of a righteous one and condemn innocent blood.

The Lord became a haven for me, and my God became the rescuer of my hope.

And he will repay their iniquity to them, and the Lord our God will obscure them according to their wickedness.[24]

O my soul, bless the Lord! O Lord my God, you were greatly exalted; you were enrobed in thanksgiving and majesty,

Putting on light as a garment, stretching out the heaven like a hide;

The one who covers his chambers in the waters, placing the clouds as his doorstep, treading upon the wings of the winds;

He who makes his messengers as spirits and his ministers a flaming fire.

Mountains go up and the plains go down into the place where you made a foundation for them;

You set a boundary which they will not pass over, nor will they return to cover the land.

You are he who commissions springs among the valleys; the waters will pass through between the mountains;

They will water all the beasts of the field, wild asses will welcome it for their thirst;

The birds of the sky will encamp upon them, they will give their voice from the midst of the rocks.

You are the one who waters the hills from his chambers; the earth will be satisfied from the fruit of your works.

It is you who raises up grass for the herds and vegetation for the service of people, to bring forth bread out of the ground;

And wine to cheer a person's heart, to brighten the face with oil; and a meal to steady a person's heart.

You placed darkness, and it became night; in it all the beasts of the forest shall come,

Even roaring young lions to seize and to seek their food from God.

The sun arose, and they were gathered

together, and they will lie down in their dens;

Man will come out to his work, and to his business until evening.

O Lord, how your works were magnified! you made all things in wisdom, the land was crammed full of your property.

This is the sea, large and broad; in it are creeping things of which there is no number, animals small and large;

The ships pass through there, this is a serpent which you made, to mock him.

All these look toward you, to give a suitable place to them.

At your giving, they will gather; yet at your opening of the hand, all things will be filled of kindness.

Yet at the turning away of your face, they will be troubled; you will take away their breath, and they will faint and return into their dust.

You will send forth your breath; they will be created, and you will renew the face of the land.

Let the glory be the Lord's glory into the coming age, the Lord will rejoice at his works;

You are he who oversees the earth and causes it to tremble, the one who touches the hills and they smoke.

I will sing to the LORD in my life, I will strum to my God as long as I exist;

May my account be pleasing to him, yet I myself shall rejoice in the LORD.

O may sinners fail from the land, and the lawless ones as if it were not for them to exist. bless the LORD, O my soul![25]

O GOD, I expected upon you; into the coming age, may I never be turned away.

In your righteousness, rescue me and pluck me out, lean your ear toward me and liberate me!

Become for me, O God, an overshielder and a stronghold to liberate me, for you are my stability and my refuge.

O my God, rush me out of the hand of a sinner, from the hand of one who bypasses the law and causes harm;

For you, LORD, are my endurance; O Lord, you are my expectation from my youth.

I was stabilized toward you from the womb, from the belly of my mother you are my protector; my song is in you through everything.

To the many I became as a marvel, and you became as a mighty rescuer.

Let my mouth be filled with praise, so that I

would sing your glory, your majesty the whole day.

You would not fling me away in the season of old age, nor forsake me when my strength is to fail.

For my enemies spoke against me, and those who watched my soul took counsel together,

Saying, God forsook him; let us persecute and overtake him, for the one who delivers him is not.

O God, do not distance yourself from me; O my God, attend unto my rescue!

Let those who slander my soul faint and be turned back in shame; let those who seek evil things for me be clothed with shame and embarrassment.

Yet through everything I myself will expect upon you and add to all your praise.

My mouth will proclaim your righteousness and your liberation the whole day, for I sought to learn nothing higher.

I will enter in the Lord's dominion; I will be mindful of your righteousness alone, O LORD.

O God, you taught me from my youth, and even now I will recount your marvelous deeds.

And until old age and seniority, O God you would not forsake me until I declare to all the coming generation your arm, your dominion and your righteousness!

O God, the majestic things which you did are as high as the highest heights; who is like unto you, O God?

How many and harmful afflictions you showed to me; and returning, you enlivened me and brought me up again out of the depths of the ground!

Returning and multiplying your majesty, you comforted me and brought me up again out of the depths of the ground.

For to you, O God, I will acknowledge your truth with a stringed instrument; I will strum to you with a harp, O Holy One of Israel.

My lips will leap joyfully whenever I strum for you, and so will my soul which you ransomed.

Yet also will my tongue fixate the whole day upon your righteousness, when those who seek evil things for me should turn back and be embarrased.[26]

Let God arise and his enemies be scattered; and let those who hate him flee from before his face.

As smoke fades away, so let them fade away; as wax melts from the face of a fire, so may the sinners be destroyed from the face of God.

And let the righteous make merry, let them leap joyfully before God, let them gladden in merriment!

Sing to God, strum unto his name; make ye a path for him to ride upon the sunset, and leap joyfully before him—the LORD is his name. they will be troubled by his face,

The father of the orphans and judge of the widows is he; God is in his holy place.

God settles the loners in a home, leading forth the former prisoners in bravery. the ones who provoke are like those who dwell in the tombs.

O God, when you went forth before your people, when you marched through the wilderness,

     Interlude,

The land was shaken, indeed even the heavens dripped; this Sinai was shaken from the face of God, from the face of the God of Israel.

A plentiful rain, O God, you will ordain for your inheritance; and it weakened, yet you restored it.

Your creatures dwell in it; in your kindness, O God, you provided for the poor.

The chariot of God is ten thousandfold, thousands in the foremost division; God is among them, in Sinai the holy place.

You ascended into the height, you led captivity captive; you took gifts in a human, indeed to encamp even while they were unyielding.
Blessed is the LORD God.

Blessed is the Lord day by day, the God of our liberation will prosper us.

Interlude.

Our God is God to liberate; and of the
Lord GOD are the escape routes from death.

Moreover, God will shatter his enemies' heads, the scalp of hair going onward in its errors.

O God, your journeys were observed, the journeys of my God, the King who is in the holy place.

Rulers came near, having musicians in the midst of the maidens, the drummers.

Bless God in the congregations; bless the Lord from the fountains of Israel!

O God, command in your power; O God, empower this which you produced in us.

Because of your temple at Jerusalem, kings will carry gifts to you.

Rebuke the beasts of the reed; scatter the nations which desire wars! the gathering of the bulls is among the heifers of the peoples, in order for those who have been tested by silver to not be shut out.

Elders will arrive out of Egypt; Ethiopia will run forth its hand toward God.

O kingdoms of the land, sing unto God, strum unto the Lord!

       Interlude.

Strum to the one having trod upon the heaven of heaven toward the East; behold, he will give a powerful sound by his voice.

Give glory unto God; his magnificence is upon Israel, and his power is in the clouds.

Marvelous is God among his saints; the God of Israel will give power and might to his people. Blessed are you, O God![27]

Lord's Day – 1st Hour

Awake O sleeper and arise from the dead, and the Anointed King will shine upon you.[28]

Give ear to my utterances, O LORD, comprehend my cry!

Hold toward the voice of my pleading, O my King and my God; for unto you I will pray, O Lord.

Early in the morning you will hear my voice; early I will present myself to you and look up.

For you are not a God desiring lawlessness, nor will anyone who does evil dwell with you;

Lawbreakers will not remain before your eyes; you hated all those who work lawlessness.

You will destroy all those who speak falsehood; the LORD detested the man of blood and deceit.

By the richness of your rescue, I will enter into your house; in fear of you, I will bow down toward your holy temple.

O LORD, guide me in your righteousness because of my enemies; straighten your path before me.

For truth is not in their mouth; their heart is empty; a grave having been opened is their throat; by their tongues they were deceiving.

Judge them, O God; let them fall away from

their intrigues; drive them out according to the multitude of their irreverences, for they provoked you, O Lord.

But let all those who trust upon you celebrate; they will leap joyfully into the coming age, and you will settle among them, and all those who love your name will boast in you.

For you will bless the righteous one; you, LORD, will crown us as a vessel of approval.[29]

O give thanks to the LORD, for he is kind, for into the coming age is his deliverance,

Let those ransomed by the LORD speak, those whom he ransomed out of the enemy's hand;

Let them give thanks to the LORD for his deliverances and his marvelous deeds among the children of men,

For he fed the empty soul, and he filled the hungering soul with good things,

Those who sit in darkness and shadow of death, having been shackled in poverty and iron;

Let them give thanks to the LORD for his deliverances and his marvelous deeds among the children of men,

And let them sacrifice the sacrifices of thanksgiving and declare his works amid exultation.

Let them give thanks to the Lord for his deliverances and his marvelous deeds among the children of men,

Let them elevate him in the congregation of the people, and praise him in the chair of the elders.[30]

Lord's Day – 2nd Hour

I am the path and the truth and the life; no one comes toward the Father, if not through me.[31]

Judge me, O Lord, for I proceeded in my innocence, and hoping upon the Lord I will not be weakened.

Prove me and test me, O Lord, smelt my kidneys and my heart.

For your deliverance is before my eyes, and I took pleasure in your truth.

I sat not with a committee of futility, and I could not enter in with transgressors;

I hated the congregation of evildoers, and I will never sit down with the irreverent ones.

I will wash my hands in innocence and circle your altar, O Lord,

To hear the sound of praise and to recount all of your marvelous deeds.

O Lᴏʀᴅ, I loved the stature of your house, and the location of the tabernacle of your glory.

Do not destroy my soul with irreverent men, and my life with men of blood,

In whose hands are lawless actions; their right hand is crammed with gifts.

Yet I myself proceeded in my innocence; O ransom me and rescue me!

Because my foot stood in uprightness; O Lᴏʀᴅ, I will bless you in the congregations.[32]

O the depth of God's wealth and wisdom and knowledge! how unsearchable are his decisions, and untraceable are his paths!

For who knew the mind of the Lord? or who became his advisor?

Or who gave first to him and will be repaid by him?

For all things are from him and through him and for him. to him be the glory into the ages; amen![33]

Make a joyful noise to the Lᴏʀᴅ, all the earth,

Be slaves to the Lᴏʀᴅ with merriment, enter before him with joyful leaping.

Know that the Lᴏʀᴅ, he is God; he made us, and not we his people and the sheep of his pasture.

Enter into his gates amid thanksgiving, into his courtyards amid hymns; confess unto him, praise his name,

For the LORD, he is good; into the coming age is his deliverance, and into generation and generation is his truth.[34]

Lord's Day – 3rd Hour

O LORD, I will give thanks to you in my whole heart, in the council of the upright and amidst the congregation.

The works of the LORD are great; his desires for all things have been sought after;

Acknowledgement and majesty are his work, and his righteousness endures into age of age.

He made a memorial of his marvelous deeds; merciful and compassionate is the LORD.

He gave nourishment to those who fear him, he will be mindful of his covenant into the coming age.

He announced to his people the strength of his works, to give the inheritance of the nations to them.

Truth and judgment are the works of his hands; trustworthy are all his commandments,

Which have been stabilized into age of age, having been formed in truth and uprightness.

He sent a ransom for his people, he commanded his covenant into the coming age; his name is holy and formidable.

The beginning of wisdom is the fear of the LORD, a good understanding is in all those who practice it; his praise endures into age of age.[35]

Blessed is the Lord, the God of the Israel, for he visited his people and made a ransom for them,

And raised a Horn of liberation for us in the house of his servant David,

Liberation from our enemies and from the hand of all who hate us,

To make a rescue for our fathers and to remember his holy covenant,

The oath which he swore unto our father Abraham, to give to us,

Rushing us out of the hand of our enemies, to serve him fearlessly

In devotion and righteousness before him all the days of our life

Because of the compassions of the help of our God, by which the Dawnrise visited us from on high

To shine upon those sitting in darkness and in

death's shadow, to direct our feet into a path of peace.[36]

Lord's Day – 4th Hour

Blessed be the God and Father of our Master Anointed King Jesus, who according to His plentiful aid has begotten us again into a living expectation through the raising up of Anointed King Jesus out of the dead ones.

To the one being over-exceedingly able to do above all things which we request or ponder, according to the power inwardly working in us,

To him be the glory in the congregation in Anointed King Jesus into all the generations of the age of ages; amen![37]

I rejoiced at those having said to me, We will go into the house of the LORD![38]

Our Father in the heavens, your name be hallowed, your kingdom come, and your desire happen on the earth as in heaven.

Give us each day our daily bread.

And release the sins for us, because we also release for everyone obliged to us; and bring us not into testing, but rush us away from the evil one.[39]

Arise, O LORD, into your rest; you and the ark of your holiness;

Your ministers will be clothed in righteousness; your saints shall rejoice!

Because of David your slave, turn not away the face of your Anointed.

The LORD swore a truth to David and will not displace it: I will place upon your throne from the fruit of your womb;

There I will sprout up a horn for David, I prepared a lamp for my Anointed.

I will clothe his enemies in shame, but my holiness shall blossom forth upon him.[40]

Holy, holy, holy is the Lord God the Omnipotence, who was and is and is coming.

Let there be glory and honor and gratitude to the one sitting upon the throne, he who lives into the ages of ages,

Worthy are you the Holy One, our Master and God, to take the glory and the honor and the the power; for you created all things, and they existed and were created because of your will![41]

Lord's Day – 5th Hour

Blessed are the poor in spirit, for theirs is the

kingdom of the heavens.

Blessed are those who grieve, for they will be encouraged.

Blessed are the meek, for they will inherit the land.

Blessed are those who hunger and thirst for righteousness, for they shall be satisfied.

Blessed are those who rescue, for they will be rescued.

Blessed are the clean in heart, for they will see God.

Blessed are those who make peace, for they shall be called God's children.

Blessed those having been persecuted because of righteousness, for theirs is the kingdom of the heavens.[42]

The LORD is my light and my liberator; whom shall I fear? the LORD is the overshielder of my life; of whom shall I be frightened?

While the evildoers—my enemies and those who afflict me—were approaching me to consume my flesh, they became weak and they fell;

If an encampment should mobilize toward me, my heart will not fear; if a battle should arise against me, in this I hope.

One thing I asked from the LORD, I will seek after this, to dwell in the house of the LORD all the days of my life, to observe the pleasantness of the LORD, and to look upon his temple.

For he hid me in a tent in the day of my troubles; he sheltered me in the covering of his tabernacle, he uplifted me in the rock;

And now behold, he uplifted my head over my enemies; I circled in his tabernacle and sacrificed the sacrifice of a joyful noise, I will sing and strum before the LORD.

O LORD, listen closely to the voice which I cried out; rescue me and hear from me!

My heart said to you: He sought my face; O LORD, I will seek your face.

You would not turn your countenance away from me; you would not bend away from your slave in anger; become my rescuer! O God my liberator, you would not expel me nor forsake me.

For my father and my mother forsook me, yet the LORD received me.

O LORD, ordain me in your path, and guide me in a straight track for the sake of my enemies.

Deliver me not into the souls who afflict me, for unjust witnesses arose against me; injustice even lied to itself.

I trust to see the good things of the LORD in the land of living.

O await for the LORD; be valorous and let your heart be strengthened, and wait upon the LORD![43]

Lord's Day – 6th Hour

And likewise the Spirit assists in our weaknesses; for we have not perceived what we should necessarily pray about, but the same Spirit super-intercedes on our behalf in unutterable groanings [44]

Halleluia! praise the LORD. praise the name of the LORD, O ye slaves

Who have stood in the house of the LORD, in the courtyards of the house of our God.

Praise the LORD, for the LORD is good; strum unto his name, for it is beautiful;

For the LORD set apart Jacob to himself, and Israel for his peculiar treasure.

For I knew that great is the LORD and our Master compared to all the gods;

All things, as many as the LORD desired, he made in the sky and in the land, in the seas and in all the depths;

Bringing up clouds out of the ends of the land,

he made lightnings for the rain; it is he who brings forth the winds from his treasuries.

O LORD, into the coming age is your name, O LORD, your remembrance continues into generation and generation.[45]

Even until the present hour we hunger and thirst and go naked and roam and are beaten;

And we tire, working with our own hands; being insulted, we bless; being persecuted, we endure, being despised, we encourage;

We were made to become like the abhorrences of the world, the scum of all things until the present time.[46]

Halleluia! praise God among his saints, praise him in the steadfastness of his power.

Praise him for his dominant deeds, praise him according to the magnitude of his majesty.

Praise him in a trumpet's sound, praise him in harp and lyre.

Praise him in drum and dance, praise him in strings and instrument.

Praise him with melodious cymbals, praise him with cymbals of a joyful noise.

Let every breath praise the LORD. halleluia![47]

Worthy are you to take the scroll and to open up its seals, for you were butchered, and with your blood you purchased us unto God out of every tribe and tongue and people and nation,

And you made them kings and ministers to our God; and they will reign upon the earth.

Worthy is the little Lamb, the one having been butchered, to get the power and the fullness and wisdom and strength and honor and glory and blessing.

To the One sitting upon the throne and to the little Lamb be the blessing and the honor and the glory and the might into the ages of ages![48]

Lord's Day – 7th Hour

Blessed be the God and Father of our Master Anointed King Jesus, the one regenerating us according to his powerful rescue into a living expectation through the resurrection of Anointed King Jesus from the dead;

As many as were baptized into Anointed King Jesus, we were baptized into his death

In the Name of the Father and of the Son and the Holy Spirit

The Encourager,

The Comforter,

The Exhorter, the Spirit of truth who proceeds

from the Father

And he will convict the world about sin and righteousness and judgment.

The Lord is the Spirit; yet where the Spirit of the Lord is, freedom is there.

For these are God's children, as many as are led by God's Spirit

The Spirit of adoption, in whom we cry out, Daddy Father!

The same Spirit testifies together with our spirit that we are God's offspring.

If we are offspring, also heirs, heirs of God, and co-heirs of the Anointed King if indeed we co-suffer, in order that we would also be co-glorified.

And likewise the Spirit assists in our weaknesses; for we have not perceived what we should necessarily pray about, but the same Spirit super-intercedes on our behalf in unutterable groanings[49]

Blessed is the man who proceeds not in the counsel of irreverent ones, and stands not in the path of sinful ones, and sits not on the seat of pestilent ones.

But in the law of the Lord is his desire; and in his law he preoccupies day and night.

And he will be like the tree having been planted beside inlets of waters, which gives its fruit in its season; and its leaf will not fall away; and as many things as he would do, they will all be prospered.

Not so are the irreverent ones, not so; but surely they are like the dust which the wind flings out from the face of the land.

Therefore, irreverent ones will not stand up in the judgment, nor sinful ones in the council of the righteous;

For the LORD knows the path of the righteous, and the path of the irreverent will perish.[50]

If in your mouth you confess Jesus as the Master, and trust in your heart that God raised him from the dead ones, you will be liberated;

For he is trusted in the heart for righteousness, yet he is confessed in the mouth for liberation.[51]

There is one body and one Spirit, even as you were called in one hope of your calling,

One Master, one faith, one baptism,

One God and Father of all, who is upon all and through all and within us all.[52]

Lord's Day – 8th Hour

I will bless you, O LORD, for you were angered at me, and you turned away your wrath and rescued me.

Behold, the LORD is my God and my liberator, I will be confident in him and will be liberated by him and will not be frightened; for the LORD is my glory and my praise, and he became liberation for me.

Sing of the LORD! shout his name, announce among the nations his glorious deeds, be mindful that his name has been exalted.

Sing the name of the LORD, for he made the highest things; announce these things in all the land.

Leap joyfully and make merry, ye who inhabit Zion, for the holy one of Israel is exalted in her midst![53]

And a shaft will come forth from the root of Jesse, and a bloom will ascend from the root.

And the Spirit of God will rest upon him, the Spirit of wisdom and comprehension, the Spirit of counsel and strength, the Spirit of knowledge and piety;

The Spirit of the fear of God will fill him. he will not judge according to glory nor convict according to deliberation,

But he will render judgment for the humble man and convict the humble ones of the land; and he will strike the land with the word of his mouth and shall remove an irreverent man with a breath through his lips;

And he will be girded with righteousness around his waist, and wrapped with truth around his ribs.

And a wolf will graze with a lamb, and a leopard will rest with a goat, and a calf will graze together with a bull and lion, and a little child will lead them;

And an ox and bear will graze together, and their children will be together, and a lion will eat straw together with an ox.

And an infant child will cast his hand upon the lair of serpents and upon a bed of the descendants of serpents.

And there will be in that day the root of Jesse and the one rising again to rule the nations; nations shall hope upon him, and his rest will be an honor.[54]

You are the Anointed King, the Son of the living God.[55]

Master, you are God, who made the sky and

the land and the sea and all the things in them,

The one saying through Your servant David's mouth, Why did nations rage and peoples devise vain things?

The kings of the earth stood together, and the rulers gathered together against the Lord and against his Anointed King.

For in truth, both Herod and Pontius Pilatus were gathered with nations and with the peoples of Israel against your holy Servant Jesus whom you anointed

To do as many things as your hand and your counsel predefined to happen.

Master, look upon the present things, upon their threats, and give to your slaves to speak your word with all boldness

While your hand stretches out for healing and signs and wonders to happen through the name of your holy Servant Jesus![56]

Lord's Day – 9th Hour

O LORD, our Lord, how marvelous is your name in all the earth, for your majesty is exalted above the heavens.

Out of the mouth of infants and nursing babes you prepared praise for the sake of your enemies, to dislodge an enemy and an avenger.

For I will observe the heavens, the works of your fingers, the moon and the stars which you firmly founded.

What is a man, that you are mindful of him? and the son of man, that you visit him?

For you lowered him a little compared to angels and crowned him with glory and honor;

And established him over all the works of your hands, you subjected all things below his feet,

All sheep and oxen, yet also the creatures of the plain,

The birds of the air and the fish of the sea, the things passing through the inlets of the seas.

O LORD our Lord, how marvelous is your name in all the earth![57]

Our Father in heaven, your name be hallowed,

Your kingdom come, and your will happen on earth as it does in heaven,

Give us today our daily bread,

And release for us our debts, as we ourselves also release our debtors;

And bring us not into testing, but rush us away from the evil one. for yours is the kingdom and the power and the glory into the ages; amen![58]

Save me, O LORD, for the holy one has fainted, for the faithful ones of the children of men became few.

Each one spoke useless things toward his neighbor; deceitful lips are in the heart, and by the heart they spoke.

O that the LORD would completely destroy all deceitful lips and tongues which speak lofty things,

Those who say, We will magnify our tongue, and our lips are from us; who is our master?

The LORD says, From within the misery of the poor, from the groaning of needy ones, I will now arise, I will place them in safety; I will speak boldly in it!

The oracles of the LORD are holy oracles, coins having been smelted as a trial upon the earth, having been purified sevenfold.

LORD, from this generation and into the coming age you will guard us and preserve us.

The irreverent ones walk all around; according to your stature, you will greatly care for the children of men.[59]

Lord's Day – Intercession Hour

May the LORD hear you in the day of affliction; may the name of the God of Jacob shield you.

May he dispatch aid to you from the sanctuary; and out of Zion, may he assist you.

May he be mindful of your every sacrifice and cherish your whole burnt offering.

May he give to you according to your heart and fulfill all your counsel.

We will rejoice in your liberation, and we will boast in the name of our God; may
the LORD fulfill all your requests.

Now I knew that the LORD saved his anointed one; he will heed him from his holy heaven; in his sovereignty is the liberation of his right hand.

They boast in chariots, and others in horses; yet we will boast the name of the LORD our God.

They were footbound and fell, yet we rose again and were set upright.

O LORD, save your king and heed us in the day we call upon you.[60]

Lord, come down before my little child would die![61]

O may God's peace be the umpire in your hearts, the peace into which you also were called out in one body. and you, become grateful!

May the word of the Anointed King dwell in you richly in all wisdom. teach and warn yourselves in psalms and odes and spiritual songs, singing in your heart to the Master by grace.

Everything which you would ever do in word or in work, do all things in the name of the Lord Jesus, thanking the God and Father through him.[62]

May the LORD give more to you, to you and to your children;[63]

May the God of endurance and encouragement grant to you to contemplate the same thing with one another according to Anointed King Jesus,

So that with one heart you would glorify in one mouth the God and Father of our Master, Anointed King Jesus.

May the God of anticipation cram you of all joy and peace while trusting, in order for you to overflow in anticipation in the power of the Holy Spirit.[64]

Blessed be the God and Father of our Master Anointed King Jesus, the Father of compassions and God of all encouragement,

Who encourages us in all our affliction, for us to be able to encourage people in all their affliction through the encouragement which we ourselves are encouraged by God;

For even as the sufferings of the Anointed King overflow into us, so also does our encouragement overflow through the Anointed.[65]

Siblings, may the generosity of our Master Anointed King Jesus be with your spirit; amen![66]

Lord's Day – 11th Hour

Master, toward whom will we go? you have the utterances of timeless life;

And we have trusted and known that you are the Anointed King the Son of the living God.[67]

Lord, who will sojourn in your dwelling place? who will dwell in your holy hill?

One who walks without blemish and works righteousness and speaks truth in his heart,

He who does not deceive by his tongue, nor does he do evil to his neighbor, and he does not lift an insult to those nearby him.[68]

Anointed King Jesus, who was existing in God's form, did not deem it a theft to be equal to God,

But he emptied himself, taking the form of a slave, becoming in the likeness of humans,

And being found in form as a human, he lowered himself, becoming obedient until death, yet the death of a cross.

Therefore God highly elevated him and granted to him the name above every name,

So that in the name of Jesus, every knee would bend of the heavenly ones and earthly ones and under-earth ones,

And every tongue would agree aloud that Anointed King Jesus is Master for the glory of Father God.[69]

Guard me, O Lord, for I expected upon you.

I said to the LORD, You are my Master, for you do not have a need of good things from me.

O LORD, you are the portion of my inheritance and of my cup; it is you who restores my inheritance.

The measuring lines fell for me in the best places; and indeed my inheritance is best for me.

I will bless the LORD, who gives me

understanding; indeed my inmost parts still instructed me until night.

Through everything, I was seeing the LORD before me; for he is at my right hand so that I would not be shaken.

Therefore my heart was gladdened and my tongue rejoiced, indeed even my flesh will encamp upon an expectation,

For you will not abandon my soul into hades nor give your Holy One to see decay.

You made known to me the paths of life; with your face, you will fill me with joy; in your right hand are pleasures into perfection.[70]

Amen; unto our God be the blessing and the glory and the wisdom and the gratitude and the honor and the power and the strength into ages of ages. amen![71]

Lord's Day – 12th Hour

While I was calling out, the God of my righteousness heard from me; in affliction you relieved me; O pity me and hear my prayer!

Children of men, how long will you be debased in your heart? why do you love futility and seek falsehood?

Know that the LORD also made marvelous his Holy One; the LORD will hear me when I have cried out to him.

Be moved with a passion and do not sin; speak in your hearts and be pricked upon your beds!

Sacrifice a sacrifice of righteousness, and expect upon the LORD.

Many are saying, Who will show good things to us? O LORD, the light of your face became stamped upon us.

You gave joy into my heart; they were increased from the season of their grain and wine and oil.

Together will I lie down and sleep in peace; for you, O LORD, settled me down privately with an expectation.[72]

The one who enters through the door is the shepherd of the sheep.

The doorkeeper opens up to this one, and the sheep hear his voice, and he calls his own sheep by name, and he leads them out.

Whenever he takes his own sheep, he goes before them; and the sheep listen to him, because they know his voice.

The good shepherd sets aside his life on behalf of the sheep.[73]

The LORD shepherds me, and nothing will be

lacking for me.

He encamped me in a place of green grass; he raised me up at the waters of refreshment.

He turned my soul around. he guided me upon tracks of righteousness for the sake of his name.

Even if I proceed in the midst of death's shadow, I will not fear evil things, for you yourself are with me; your rod and your staff encouraged me.

You prepared a table before me in the presence of those who afflict me; you oiled my head in oil, and your intoxicating cup was as the most powerful.

And your lovingkindness will pursue me all the days of my life, for me to dwell into length of days in the house of the LORD.[74]

We have this treasure in jars of clay, so that the supremacy of the power would be from God and not from us,

Being squeezed in everything but not crushed, being perplexed but not completely perplexed,

Being persecuted but not abandoned, being thrown down but not destroyed,

Always carrying around the death of the Master Jesus in the body, in order that the life of Jesus would also be seen in our body.

For we the living are always handed over into death on account of Jesus, so that the life of Jesus would be seen in our dying body.[75]

Second Day – 1st Hour

Awake O sleeper and arise from the dead, and the Anointed King will shine upon you.[76]

Blessed be the God and Father of our Master Anointed King Jesus, the one who blesses us in every spiritual blessing among the heavenly places in the Anointed King,

Just as before the founding of the world he also favored us in him, in order for us to be holy and blameless before him in love,

Marking us in advance, according to the good pleasure of his desire, for adoption into him through Anointed King Jesus

For the praise of the glory of his generosity with which he endowed us in the beloved one,

In whom we have the full ransom payment through his blood, the release from transgressions according to the wealth of his generosity

From which he overflowed into us in all wisdom and thoughtfulness,

Making known to us the secret of his desire, according to his good pleasure, which he exhibited in him

For an administration of the filling up of the seasons, in order to reconstitute under one head in the Anointed King all things on heaven and earth in him,

In whom we, being previously designated, were also allotted an inheritance according to an exhibition of the one who inwardly works all things according to the counsel of his desire,

So that we who have anticipated in the Anointed King would be for the praise of his glory[77]

Lord, why were the ones who afflict me multiplied? many are rising up against me;

Many are saying to my soul, There is no deliverance for him in his God.

But you, O LORD, are my helper, my glory, and lifting my head.

In my voice I screamed toward the LORD, and he heard from me out of his holy mountain.

I laid down, and I slept; I was awakened, for the LORD assisted me.

I will not be frightened from ten thousands of people, the surrounding ones who join in an attack upon me.

Rise up, O LORD, liberate me, O my God, for you struck all those who hate me pointlessly; you crushed the teeth of the sinful ones.

Liberation is of the LORD, and your blessing is

upon your people.[78]

Holy, holy, holy is the Lord God the Omnipotence, who was and is and is coming.

Let there be glory and honor and gratitude to the one sitting upon the throne, he who lives into the ages of ages,

Worthy are you the Holy One, our Master and God, to take the glory and the honor and the the power; for you created all things, and they existed and were created because of your will![79]

Second Day – 2nd Hour

Blessed be the God and Father of our Master Anointed King Jesus, the one regenerating us according to his powerful rescue into a living expectation through the resurrection of Anointed King Jesus from the dead;

As many as were baptized into Anointed King Jesus, we were baptized into his death

In the Name of the Father and of the Son and the Holy Spirit

The Encourager,

The Comforter,

The Exhorter, the Spirit of truth who proceeds from the Father

And he will convict the world about sin and righteousness and judgment.

The Lord is the Spirit; yet where the Spirit of the Lord is, freedom is there.

For these are God's children, as many as are led by God's Spirit

The Spirit of adoption, in whom we cry out, Daddy Father!

The same Spirit testifies together with our spirit that we are God's offspring.

If we are offspring, also heirs, heirs of God, and co-heirs of the Anointed King if indeed we co-suffer, in order that we would also be co-glorified.

And likewise the Spirit assists in our weaknesses; for we have not perceived what we should necessarily pray about, but the same Spirit super-intercedes on our behalf in unutterable groanings[80]

I will bless the LORD at all times, his praise shall continually be in my mouth.

My soul makes its boast in the LORD; let the meek ones hear and rejoice.

O magnify the LORD with me, and let us exalt his name together.

I sought out the LORD, and he heard from me,

and delivered me from all of my wanderings.

Come unto him and be illuminated, and your faces could never be ashamed.

Taste and see that the LORD is good; blessed is a man who expects in him.

Fear the LORD, O his holy ones, for nothing is lacking to those who fear him.

Near is the LORD to those having been crushed in heart; and he will liberate those who are lowly in spirit.

Many are the afflictions of the righteous, and he will deliver them from them all.

The LORD guards all their bones; not one of them shall be crushed.

The LORD will ransom the souls of his slaves, and those who expect upon him could not be in disharmony.[81]

Second Day – 3rd Hour

Let my mouth be filled with praise, so that I would sing your glory and your majesty the whole day![82]

In the beginning was the Word, and the Word was with God, and the Word was God.

This one was being in the beginning with God.

all things became through him, and apart from

him nothing became which has become.

Life was in him, and the life was the light of humans.

The light shines amid darkness, and darkness did not overtake it.

He was the true light which illuminates every human coming into the world.

He was being in the world, and the world became through him, and the world did not know him.

He came into his own things, and his own people did not accept him.

As many as took him, those who trust in his name, to them he gave the authority to become God's offspring

Who were not generated from blood, nor from a desire of flesh, nor from the desire of a man, but from God.

The Word became flesh and encamped among us; and we beheld his glory, glory as of the only-begotten from the Father, crammed of generosity and truth.

We all took from his fullness, even generosity for generosity;

Because the law was given through Moses, yet generosity and truth happened through Anointed King Jesus.[83]

The law of the LORD is spotless, turning around the soul; the testimony of the LORD is trustworthy, making childish ones wise;

The statutes of the LORD are upright, cheering the heart; the commandment of the LORD is radiant, illuminating the eyes.

The fear of the LORD is holy, enduring into age of age; the judgments of the LORD are true, having been altogether justified,

And desired more than gold and much precious stone, and sweeter than honey and the honeycomb.

Indeed your servant guards them; there is much reward in guarding them.

Who will recognize missteps? cleanse me from my hidden things.

Spare your slave from strange things; if they would not take mastery over me, then I will be spotless and be cleansed from great sin.

And the words of my mouth and the meditation of my heart will always be a good pleasure before you, O LORD, my rescuer and my ransomer![84]

Second Day – 4th Hour

We give thanks to the Father who enables us for the portion of the inheritance of the saints in light,

He who rushed us out of the authority of darkness and transferred us into the kingdom of his beloved Son,

In whom we have the ransom payment, the release from sins;

Who is the icon of the invisible God, the

firstborn of all creation,

For all things were created by him, the things in the heavens and the things upon the earth, the visible and invisible things,

Whether thrones or lordships, whether rulers or authorities, all things were created through him and for him,

And he is before all things, and all things have taken shape in him,

And he is the head of the body, the congregation; he who is the beginning, the firstborn out of the dead, in order that he would become foremost in all things

Because all the fullness was pleased to dwell in him

And through him to fully change all things for him, making peace through the blood of his cross; all things through him, whether things on earth or in the heavens.[85]

O Lᴏʀᴅ, the king will rejoice in your strength; and greatly he will leap for joy at your liberation!

You gave to him the passion of his soul and deprived not the desire of his lips.

For you ran before him in blessings of kindness; you placed upon his head a crown of precious stone.

Life he asked of you, and you gave to him length of days into age of age.

His glory is great amidst your liberation; you placed upon him glory and majesty;

For you will give a blessing to him into age of age; with your face you will cheer him with gladness.

For the king expects upon the Lᴏʀᴅ; and he could not possibly be shaken amidst the lovingkindness of the most High.

May your hand be found by all your enemies; may your right hand find all those who hate you.

Be uplifted, O Lᴏʀᴅ, in your power; and we will sing and strum about your dominant deeds![86]

Certainly I consider all things to be a loss because of the superiority of the knowledge of my Master Anointed King Jesus, on account of whom I have lost all things; and I consider all things to be dung so that I would gain the Anointed King

And be found in him—not having my righteousness from the law, but having through a trust of the Anointed King the righteousness from God which exists upon trust—

In order to know him and to know the power of his resurrection and to know the sharing of his sufferings, being conformed to his death[87]

Second Day – 5th Hour

If the Lord would not construct the house, those who construct it toil for futility. if the Lord would not guard the city, the watchman stays awake for uselessness.[88]

Why do I fear in an evil day? the lawlessness at my heel will encircle me.

As for those who have taken confidence in their power and who boast upon the multitude of their wealth,

A sibling does not ransom them; will a human pay the ransom? he will not give to God his satisfaction

And the price of his soul's ransom.

He ceased into the coming age and shall live into the end, for he will not see corruption when he sees the wise ones dying.

Thoughtless and mindless ones will perish together and abandon their wealth to strangers,

But God will ransom my soul from the hand of hades when he should receive me.[89]

Having anciently spoken by the prophets many times and in many ways to the fathers, God at these last days spoke to us in the Son,

Whom he placed as heir of all things, and through whom he made the ages,

Who—being the radiance of the glory and the imprint of his subsistence, also bearing all things in the utterance of his power—when he had made through himself a cleansing of our sins, he sat down in the right hand of the Majesty in high places[90]

O LORD, your lovingkindness is in the sky; and your truth as far as the clouds.

Your righteousness is as the mountains of God, your judgments are a vast deep; O LORD, you will heal humans and beasts.

O God, how you multiplied your aid! the children of men will hope in the shelter of your wings.

They will be intoxicated from the fatness of your house, and you will water them with the river of your luxury.

For in your presence is a fountain of life; in your light we will see light.

Extend your aid to those who know you; and your righteousness to the upright in heart.

Let a foot of pride not come unto me, and let the hand of sinners shake me not![91]

Rabbi, you are the Son of God; you are the King of Israel!

Yes Lord, I have trusted that you are the Anointed King, the Son of God, the one coming into the world.

Master, I will journey with you to wherever you would go.[92]

Second Day – 6th Hour

Unti you O LORD I cried out: O my God, you would not pass me by silently, lest silently you might pass from me and I would become like those who go down into the pit.

O hear from the voice of my pleading when I plead unto you, while uplifting my hands toward your holy temple.

You should not draw together my soul with

sinful ones, nor destroy me with those who work injustice, who speak peace to their neighbors, yet misdeeds are in their hearts.

Give to them according to their works and according to the wickedness of their pursuits; give to them according to the works of their hands; repay their repayment to them.

For they did not meditate in the works of the LORD and in the works of his hands; you will tear them down and never build them up.

O blessed be the LORD, for he listened closely to the sound of my pleading.

The LORD is my rescuer and my overshielder; my heart expected upon him, and I was rescued, and my body sprouted anew; and I will sing praise to him from my own desire.

The LORD is the power of his people, and he is an overshielder of the salvation of his anointed.

O liberate your people and bless your heritage, and shepherd them and uplift them until the coming age.[93]

Bring to the LORD, O children of God, bring glory and honor to the LORD.

Bring to the LORD glory unto his name; worship the LORD in his holy court!

The voice dividing a flame of fire is of the LORD,

The voice shaking the wilderness is of the LORD, and the LORD will shake the wilderness of Kadesh.

The voice preparing a deer is of the LORD, and he will uncover thickets; and in his temple everyone speaks glory.

The LORD will give strength to his people; the LORD will bless his people in peace![94]

Jesus also suffered outside of the gate so that he might hallow the people through his own blood.

So we should now come out toward him outside of the encampment, bearing his reproach;

For we do not have a city remaining here, but we seek out the city which will be.

Therefore through him we should offer to God a sacrifice of praise in everything, this is a fruit from lips agreeing unto his name.[95]

To the One loving us and washing us from our sins in his blood, Anointed King Jesus, the trustworthy witness, the first born from the dead, and the Ruler of the kings of the earth,

Into ages of ages, let the glory and the power be unto him who made us a kingdom, as ministers unto his God and Father; amen.[96]

Second Day – 7th Hour

O the desolate places of Jerusalem, burst forth in rejoicing, for the LORD had compassion upon Jerusalem and delivered her!

The LORD unveiled his holy arm in the sight of all the nations, and all the ends of the earth will see the salvation which comes from the presence of God.

Depart, depart, ye who carry the vessels of the LORD! come out from there and touch not an unclean thing; come out and be separated from her midst;

For you will not leave in commotion nor will you go in retreat, because the LORD will go before you; and he who gathers you will be the LORD God of Israel.

Behold, my servant will understand and be exalted and glorified greatly.

Many people were shocked at you, and so shall your appearance be despised away from men, and your glory from the people,

In this way will many nations marvel at him, and kings will constrain their mouth; for they to whom it was not announced concerning him will see, and those who have not heard will comprehend.

LORD, who trusted our report? and to whom was the arm of the LORD unveiled?

We announced before him who was as a child, like a root in a thirsting land, in whom there is no form nor glory; and we saw him, and he had no form nor beauty;

But his form was without honor, failing compared to all people, a man being in calamity and having known how to bear weakness, for his face was turned away; he was dishonored and not accounted.

This one bears our sins and is pained for us, and we accounted him to be in hardship and in calamity and in oppression.

Yet he was wounded because of our transgressions and was weakened because of our sins; the chastisement of our peace was upon him, we were healed by his bruising.

We all strayed like sheep, humanity strayed in his path; and the LORD gave him over for our sins.

And he, on account of having been harmed, did not open his mouth; he was led as a sheep to slaughter; and as a lamb is silent before its shearers, so he does not open his mouth.

In his humiliation, his judgment was lifted; who will recount his generation? for his life was lifted from the land, he was led into death because of the transgressions of my people.

And I will give the evildoers for his burial and the wealthy for his death; because he committed not transgression, neither was deceit found in his mouth.

And the LORD desires to cleanse him of the wound—if you would give concerning sin, your soul will see a long lived seed—and the LORD desires to lift it away

From the toil of his life, to show light by him and to shape it in the understanding, to justify the righteous one who serves well as a slave for the many; and he himself shall bear their sins.

Therefore he will inherit many and will divide the spoils of the strong for whom his life was given over into death and was reckoned among the lawless ones; and he himself bore the sins of many and was given over on account of their sins.[97]

Second Day – 8th Hour

Blessed be the God and Father of our Master Anointed King Jesus, the one regenerating us according to his powerful rescue into a living expectation through the resurrection of Anointed King Jesus from the dead;

As many as were baptized into Anointed King Jesus, we were baptized into his death

In the Name of the Father and of the Son and the Holy Spirit

The Encourager,

The Comforter,

The Exhorter, the Spirit of truth who proceeds from the Father

And he will convict the world about sin and righteousness and judgment.

The Lord is the Spirit; yet where the Spirit of the Lord is, freedom is there.

For these are God's children, as many as are led by God's Spirit

The Spirit of adoption, in whom we cry out, Daddy Father!

The same Spirit testifies together with our spirit that we are God's offspring.

If we are offspring, also heirs, heirs of God, and co-heirs of the Anointed King if indeed we co-suffer, in order that we would also be co-glorified.

And likewise the Spirit assists in our weaknesses; for we have not perceived what we should necessarily pray about, but the same Spirit super-intercedes on our behalf in unutterable groanings[98]

Blessed are those whose lawless deeds were released, whose sins were covered;

Blessed is the man to whom the LORD could not account sin, neither is there any deceit in his mouth.

Because I kept silence, my bones aged from my crying out all day long;

For your hand weighed down day and night upon me; I was turned for misery when a thorn was being implanted.

I made known my sin, and I did not concealed my lawlessness; I said, Against myself I will declare my lawlessness to the LORD; and you released me from the irreverence of my sin.

Every saint will pray to you over this in the proper season; but the waters will not come near to him amid a deluge of many waters.

You yourself are my refuge from the affliction which encompasses me; O my exultation, ransom me from those who encircle me!

Many are the scourges of the sinful person; yet lovingkindness will encircle the one who expects upon the LORD.

Be gladdened before the LORD and leap for joy, ye righteous ones; and rejoice, all ye who are upright in heart![99]

Great and marvelous are your works, Lord God Omnipotence. righteous and true are your paths, O King of the nations.

Lord, who could not fear and glorify your name? for you alone are pure, for all the nations will arrive and bow down before you, for your decrees were made visible.[100]

Second Day – 9th Hour

Our soul endures in the LORD, for he is our rescuer and overshielder;

For in him our heart will be gladdened, and we placed expectation in his holy name.

O LORD, just as we expected upon you, may your lovingkindness happen for us.[101]

Everyone who trusts that Jesus is the Anointed King, he has been generated from God, and everyone who loves the generating one also loves each one who was generated from him.

We know that we love God's children by this, when we love God and guard his commands.

For the love of God is this, so that we would guard his commands. and his commands are not heavy,

Because everyone having been generated from God conquers the world; and our trust is this conquest which conquers the world.

Who is the one conquering the world, except the one who trusts that Jesus is the Son of God?

This Anointed King Jesus is the one coming through water and blood, not in the water alone, but in the water and the blood; and the Spirit is testifying, because the Spirit is the truth.

For three are those who testify in heaven, the Father, the Word and the Holy Spirit, and these three are one; three also are the ones testifying in the earth,

The Spirit and the water and the blood; and the three are for the one testimony.

If we take the testimony of people, God's testimony is greater because the testimony of God is this which he has testified about his Son.

He who trusts into the Son of God has the testimony in him; yet he who does not trust in God has made him a liar, for he has not trusted in the testimony which God has testified about his Son.

This is the testimony, it is that God has given

timeless life to us; and this life is in his Son.

He who has the Son has the life; the one who does not have the Son of God does not have the life.[102]

I said I will guard my pathways, to not sin with my tongue; I will set a guard over my mouth when the sinner arrays himself before me.

LORD, make known to me what is my end and the number of my days, so that I would know what I am lacking.

Lo, you appointed my days like the widths of a hand, and my age is as nothing before you; moreover, every living person does all things out of futility.

Nevertheless each person passes through in a pattern, moreover they are troubled for nothing; someone stores away treasures and knows not for whom he will gather them.

And now what is my endurance? is it not you, O Lord? even my existence is from you.

Rush me away from all my lawless deeds! you gave me opportunity to be a disgrace even to the senseless person.

O LORD, listen closely to my prayer and give ear to my pleading! do not pass by silently from my tears, for I myself am a stranger before you and a sojourner like all my fathers.[103]

Second Day – Intercession Hour

For this reason I bend my knees toward the Father of our Master Anointed King Jesus,

From whom every paternal lineage is named in heaven and on earth,

So that according to the wealth of his glory he would grant unto you to be invigorated in power through his Spirit in the inner human,

In order for the Anointed King to dwell in your hearts through trust,

Having been rooted and founded in love so that you would fully prevail, to grasp with all the saints what is the width and length and depth and height of this love,

And to know the love of the Anointed King which goes beyond knowledge, in order that you would be filled into all the fullness of God.[104]

Blessed are the poor in spirit, for theirs is the kingdom of the heavens.

Blessed are those who grieve, for they shall be encouraged.

Blessed are the meek, for they will inherit the land.

Blessed are those who hunger and thirst for righteousness, for they shall be satisfied.

Blessed are those who rescue, for they will be rescued.

Blessed are the clean in heart, for they will see God.

Blessed are those who make peace, for they shall be called God's children.

Blessed those having been persecuted because of righteousness, for theirs is the kingdom of the heavens.[105]

I lifted my eyes into the hills. from where does my rescue arrive?

My rescue is from the LORD who made the heaven and the earth.

He would not give your foot into shaking, nor would he lull to sleep the one who guards you.

Behold, he who guards Israel will neither tire nor slumber.

The LORD guards you, the LORD is your shelter at your right hand.

The sun will not enflame you by day, nor will the moon enflame the night.

The LORD will guard you from every evil; he will guard your soul.

The LORD will guard your entryway and your

exit-way from now and until age to come.[106]

Second Day – 11th Hour

Waiting I waited for the LORD, and he heeded me and listened closely to my pleading,

And he brought me up from a pit of misery and from a mire of slime, and he stood my feet upon a rock and straightened my steps,

And he hurled a new song into my mouth, a hymn unto our God: Many will see, and fear, and expect upon the LORD.

Blessed is the man whose expectation is the name of the LORD, and he did not gaze at futilities and false ravings.

O LORD my God, you made many things, your marvelous works; and in regard to your thoughts, there is none who will be compared to you. I declared it and said, They prevailed beyond number!

Sacrifice and offering you did not desire, yet you prepared a body for me. you requested not a whole burnt offering and sin offering.

Then said I, Behold I have come, in the tip of a scroll it has been written about me:

O my God, I wanted in the midst of my stomach to do your desire and your law.

In a great congregation, I evangelized

righteousness; lo, I could not stop my lips. you knew it, O LORD.

I did not conceal your righteousness in my heart, I spoke your truth and your liberation, I did not conceal your lovingkindness and your truth from a large gathering.

Yet you, O LORD, would not distance your compassions from me; your lovingkindness and your truth assisted me through everything.

For evil things beyond number encompassed me; my lawless deeds overtook me, and I was not able to see; they were multiplied more than the hairs of my head, and my heart abandoned me.

O LORD, be pleased to deliver me; O LORD, take heed to rescue me!

O may they be ashamed and embarrassed who seek my soul to remove it; may they be turned backwards and be embarrassed who desire evil things for me.

Let them obtain their shame who say to me, Well done, well done!

May all those who seek you be gladdened and rejoice before you, and let those who love your liberation say through everything: The LORD be magnified!

Yet I myself am poor and needy; the Lord will

take thought of me; you are my rescuer and my overshielder; O my God, you would not delay.[107]

Vindicate me, O God, and determine my justice from an unholy nation; rush me away from the deceitful and unjust person.

For you yourself are my strength, O God; why do you drive me away? And why do I go moping while my enemy presses me out?

Dispatch your light and your truth; let them guide me and lead me into your holy hill and to your tabernacles!

And I will enter before the altar of God, before the God who gladdens my youthfulness; I will sing praise to you with a harp, O God my God.

O my soul, why are you all sorrowful? and why agitate me? hope upon God! for I will sing praise to him; my God is the liberation of my countenance.[108]

Second Day – 12th Hour

How long, O LORD, will you completely forget me? how long will you turn away your face from me?

Until when will I appoint deliberations in my soul, daily pains in my heart? how long will my enemy be uplifted above me?

Look closely, O Lᴏʀᴅ, hear from me, O my God; enlighten my eyes, lest I should slumber into death,

Lest my enemy should say, I prevailed toward him! those who afflict me will rejoice if ever I be shaken.

Yet I expected upon your rescue, my heart will leap joyfully at your liberation; I will sing to the Lᴏʀᴅ who does well unto me, and I will strum to the name of the Lord, the most High![109]

Yes, amen; come, Lord Jesus!

The generosity of the Master Anointed King Jesus be with all the saints; amen![110]

Hear from my righteousness, O Lᴏʀᴅ, take heed of my pleading, give ear to my prayer which is not in lips of deceit.

O may my judgment come forth from your face; let my eyes perceive upright deeds!

You proved my heart, you visited in the night; by fire you refined me, and unrighteousness was not found in me.

I kept the hard roads because of the words of your lips, so that my mouth would never utter the works of men.

Repair my steps in your paths, so that my steps would not be shaken.

O God, I cried out because you listened; incline your ear to me, and take heed of my utterances.

Show marvelously your tender mercies; as for those who expect upon you, you liberate them from those who oppose your right hand.

Guard me like the pupil of an eye! you will shelter me in the shelter of your wings

From the face of the irreverent ones who distress me. my enemies encircled my soul;

They locked up their stubbornness; their mouth spoke arrogance.

Throwing me out, they presently encircled me; they appointed their eyes to bend toward the ground.

They seize me like a lion prepared for the chase and like a young lion who dwells in hidden places.

Rise up, O LORD, outrun them and topple them down; deliver my soul from irreverent ones, and your sword from the enemies of your hand!

O LORD, separate them in their life from a few things of the earth. even their womb was filled of your hidden things, they were satisfied of children, and they left the remaining things to their babes.

Yet as for me, I will be seen before your face in righteousness; I will be satisfied when your glory is revealed.[111]

Third Day – 1ˢᵗ Hour

Awake O sleeper and arise from the dead, and the Anointed King will shine upon you.[112]

Rescue me, O God; rescue me, for my soul has yielded to you! and I will hope in the shadow of your wings until lawlessness should pass by.

I will cry out unto God the most High, the God who does well to me.

He sent forth from heaven, and he liberated me; he gave into contempt those who trample me. God sent forth his rescue and his truth,

And he rushed my soul from the midst of young lions. I laid down having been troubled; the teeth of the children of men hold a weapon and arrows, and their tongue is a sharp sword.

O God, be exalted over the skies, and your glory over all the land!

They prepared a trap for my feet, and they bent down my soul; they dug a pit before my face and fell into it.

My heart is ready, O God, ready is my heart; I will sing and strum.

O my glory, wake up! psaltery and harp, wake up! early I shall wake up.

I will sing praise to you among the peoples, O Lord; I will strum to you among the nations,

For your rescue was magnified to the skies, and
your truth unto the clouds.

Be exalted above the skies, O God, and your
glory over all the land![113]

O LORD my God, I expected upon you; rescue
me and liberate me from all those who
persecute me,

Lest he should snatch away my soul like a lion,
while no one ransoms or liberates.

Arise in your anger, O LORD, be lifted up amid
the limitations of my enemies; awaken, O Lord
my God, in the decree which you commanded!

A gathering of peoples will encircle you; return
into the height for their sake.

The LORD will judge the peoples; judge me,
O LORD, according to my righteousness and
according to my innocence in me.

Let the wickedness of sinful ones be ended!
you will make the righteous one upright, O
God, testing the hearts and inmost parts.

Righteous is my rescue from God, who
liberates the upright in heart.

God is the judge, righteous and strong and
longsuffering, not bringing up anger each day.

I will sing praise to the LORD according to his
righteousness, and I will strum to the name of

the LORD the most High.[114]

Third Day – 2nd Hour

As many as were baptized into Anointed King Jesus, we were baptized into his death.

Therefore we were buried together with him through baptism into death; so that just as the Anointed King was roused from the dead ones through the Father's glory, in this way we too should walk in novelty of life.

For if we have become planted together in the likeness of his death, yet also of the resurrection will we be,

Knowing this, that our old person was crucified together, in order that the body of sin would be shut down, for us to no longer a slave to sin;

For the one who dies has been made righteous away from sin.

If we died together in the Anointed King, we trust that we will also live together in him,

Having perceived that the Anointed King, being awakened out of the dead, no longer dies; death no longer masters him.

For which death he died, he died once only unto sin; yet which thing he lives, he lives unto God.

As many as were baptized in the Anointed King

have put on the Anointed King.[115]

Give ear, O God, to my prayer, and do not overlook my pleading.

Attend to me and listen closely to me. in my pondering, I was grieved and agitated

By the enemy's voice and the affliction from a sinful person; for they bent lawlessness toward me, and they were spiting me in anger.

My heart was stirred within me, and the terror of death fell upon me;

Fearfulness and trembling came upon me, and darkness covered me.

And I said, Who will give me wings like a dove, and I will fly and rest?

Behold, fleeing I went afar and encamped in the wilderness.

I was anticipating the one who liberates me from discouragement and storms.

O Lord, drown and disperse their tongues, for I saw lawlessness and disputing in the city.

Yet as for me, I cried aloud unto God, and the LORD listened closely to me.

Evening and early and midday will I recount; I shall report, and he will listen closely to my voice.

He will ransom my soul in peace from those

who approach me, for they were among the many with me.

God will listen closely and humble them, he who exists before the ages. for there is no change in them, and they did not fear God.[116]

Third Day – 3rd Hour

Blessed be the God and Father of our Master Anointed King Jesus, the one regenerating us according to his powerful rescue into a living expectation through the resurrection of Anointed King Jesus from the dead;

As many as were baptized into Anointed King Jesus, we were baptized into his death

In the Name of the Father and of the Son and the Holy Spirit

The Encourager,

The Comforter,

The Exhorter, the Spirit of truth who proceeds from the Father

And he will convict the world about sin and righteousness and judgment.

The Lord is the Spirit; yet where the Spirit of the Lord is, freedom is there.

For these are God's children, as many as are led by God's Spirit

The Spirit of adoption, in whom we cry out,

Daddy Father!

The same Spirit testifies together with our spirit that we are God's offspring.

If we are offspring, also heirs, heirs of God, and co-heirs of the Anointed King if indeed we co-suffer, in order that we would also be co-glorified.

And likewise the Spirit assists in our weaknesses; for we have not perceived what we should necessarily pray about, but the same Spirit super-intercedes on our behalf in unutterable groanings[117]

As the deer yearns for springs of waters, so does my soul long for you, O God.

My soul thirsted for the living God. when will I arrive and appear before God?

My tears became my food day and night while each day it was said to me, Where is your God?

I was mindful of these things, and I poured out my soul upon me, for I will pass through in the place of a marvelous tabernacle as far as the house of God, in a voice of exultation and thanksgiving amid the sound of a festival celebration!

Why are you all sorrowful, O my soul, and why do you agitate me? expect upon God, for I will acknowledge him! O my God, you are the liberation of my countenance.

My soul was disturbed at myself; therefore I will be mindful of you from the land of Jordan and Hermon, from a small mountain.

Deep calls unto deep for the sound of your waterfalls; all your surges and your waves came through upon me.

By day the LORD will command his lovingkindness, and by night a song will be with me, my prayer to the God of my life.

I will say to God, You are my helper; why did you forget me? why do I go moping when my enemy causes affliction?

While crushing my bones, my enemies reviled me by their saying to me daily, Where is your God?

Why are you all sorrowful, O my soul, and why do you agitate me? expect upon God, for I will acknowledge him! you, O my God, are the liberation of my countenance.[118]

Third Day – 4th Hour

Amen, halleluiah! praise our God, all ye his slaves and those who fear him, great and small.

Halleluiah, for the Lord God the Omnipotence reigns!

Blessed are those who have been called into the supper of the wedding of the little Lamb![119]

My heart blurted out a good word, my verses I recite for the king, my tongue is the pen of a quick scribe.

A ripe beauty are you compared to the children of men, favor was poured out in your lips; therefore God blessed you into the coming age.

O mighty one, wrap your sword around your thigh in your ripeness and your beauty,

And stretch forth and prosper and reign on account of truth and meekness and righteousness; and your right hand will guide you marvelously.

O mighty one, your sharpened arrows are in the hearts of the king's enemies; the peoples will fall beneath you.

Into age of age is your throne, O God; the rod of your kingdom is a rod of uprightness.

You loved righteousness and hated lawlessness; therefore God your God anointed you with the oil of gladness beside your companions.

From your garments from ivory towers are cassia and myrrh and oil of myrrh with which they brought you merriment.

Daughters of kings were in honor of you; at your right hand stood the queen wrapped in apparel having been embroidered in golden weaving.

O daughter, listen and behold and incline your ear, and forget your people and the house of your father,

For the king greatly desired your beauty, for he himself is your Master.

Even the daughters of Tyre bowed down to him among gifts; the wealthy ones of the people will intreat your face.

All the same glory of the king's daughter is wrapped within, having been embroidered in gold fringed garments.

Virgins will be led behind her to the king, her companions will be brought before you;

They will be led in merriment and joyful leaping, they shall be brought into the king's palace.

Instead of your fathers, children became yours; you will appoint them as rulers over all the land.

I will be mindful of your name in every generation and generation; therefore the peoples will sing praise unto you into the coming age and into age of age.[120]

To the only wise God our liberator be glory and majesty, might and authority, even now and into all the ages; amen![121]

Third Day – 5th Hour

God is our refuge and power; during the afflictions befalling us, greatly is he a rescuer.

Therefore we will not fear when the land is shaken and mountains are removed into the hearts of the seas.

The LORD of armies is with us, the God of Jacob is our overshielder.

He will crush the bow and shatter the weapon and burn down the shields with fire, canceling wars as far as the extremities of the earth.

Be still and know that I myself am God; I will be exalted in the nations, I will be exalted in the earth.

The LORD of hosts is with us, the God of Jacob is our overshielder.[122]

Amen; unto our God be the blessing and the glory and the wisdom and the gratitude and the honor and the power and the strength into ages of ages. amen![123]

It is a good thing to give thanks to the LORD, and to strum to your name, O Most High,

To announce your lovingkindness in the morning, and your faithfulness each night

By a ten-stringed instrument with a song in a lyre.

For you, LORD, did gladden me by your action, and I will rejoice in the works of your hands.

O LORD, how your works were magnified! your calculations penetrated deeply with precision.

An imprudent man will not know, and an uncomprehending one will not comprehend these things.

When the sinners were to sprout up like the grass, all the workers of lawlessness also watched closely, so they would perish for age of age.

Yet into the coming age, O LORD, you are the most High;

For behold, your enemies will perish, and all those who work lawlessness will be dispersed,

And my horn will be exalted like a unicorn, and my old age in glistening oil,

Even among my enemies, my eye oversaw; even among the evildoers who rise up against me, my ear will hear!

The righteous one will bloom like a palm tree,

he will be multiplied as if a cedar in Lebanon.

Those who have been planted in the house of the LORD will bloom forth in the courts of our God;

In glistening old age, they will still prevail and be constantly rejoicing

To announce that the LORD my God is upright, there is not an injustice in him![124]

Third Day – 6th Hour

Amid my pleading, O God, listen closely to my voice; remove my soul away from the fear of the enemy.

You sheltered me from the conspiring of evildoers, from the multitude of those who work lawlessness.[125]

Great and marvelous are your works, Lord God Omnipotent. righteous and true are your paths, O King of the nations.

Lord, who could not fear and glorify your name? for you alone are pure, for all the nations will arrive and bow down before you, for your decrees became apparent.[126]

Our Father in heaven, your name be hallowed,

Your kingdom come, and your will happen on earth as it does in heaven,

Give us today our daily bread,

And release for us our debts, as we ourselves also release our debtors;

And bring us not into testing, but rush us away from the evil one. for yours is the kingdom and the power and the glory into the ages; amen![127]

Judge, O LORD, those who harm me; make war against those who war against me.

Seize a weapon and a shield, and rise up for my rescue,

Draw forth a sword, and enclose me from before those who persecute me; say unto my soul: Your liberation I am.

Let those who seek my soul be ashamed and embarrassed; let them be turned away and entirely ashamed who account evils unto me.

Let them become like dust against a wind, and with an angel of the LORD afflicting them!

All my bones will utter, O LORD who is like unto you who rushes a poor person out of the hand of his hardened foe, even a poor and needy person from those who plunder him?

The whole day my tongue will also attend to your righteousness and to your praise.[128]

My soul magnifies the Lord

And my spirit has rejoiced in God my liberator,

For he looked upon the lowliness of his slave.

For the powerful one did great things for me, and holy is his name.

And his mercy is for generations of generations to those who fear him.

He performed mighty deeds by his arm, he scattered haughty ones in the thinking of their hearts.

He took down rulers from thrones and elevated the lowly ones.

He filled hungering ones of good things, and those who were being enriched he sent out empty.[129]

Third Day – 7th Hour

Aid me, O God, according to your great aid, and wipe out my transgression according to the plenitude of your pity;

Wash me thoroughly from my lawlessness, and cleanse me from my sin.

For I know my lawlessness, and my sin is always before me.

Against you alone did I sin, and I did this evil thing before you, in such a manner that you would be justified in your words and triumph in your judging.

For behold, I was conceived in lawlessness; and in sin my mother conceived me.

For behold, you loved truth, you clarified for me the unclear and concealed things of your wisdom.

You will sprinkle me with hyssop, and I shall be cleansed; you will wash me, and I will be whitened more than snow.

You will cause me to hear exultation and merriment; the humbled bones will leap joyfully.

Turn your face away from my sins, and wipe out all my lawless deeds.

Create a pure heart in me, O God, and renew an upright spirit in my bowels.

You should not cast your face away from me and remove your Holy Spirit from me.

O render unto me the great joy of your liberation, and stabilize me in a governing spirit.

I will teach lawless ones your paths, and the irreverent will turn back toward you.

Rush me away from bloodshed, O God the God of my liberation! my tongue will celebrate your righteousness.

O Lord, you will unlock my lips, and my mouth will announce your praise.

For if you desired a sacrifice, I would have given it; whole burnt offering you did not find pleasing.

A sacrifice to God, a spirit having been broken, a heart having been broken and humbled, O God, you will not disregard these.[130]

Great and exceedingly praiseworthy is the LORD in the city of our God, in his holy mountain.

O God, we considered your lovingkindness in the midst of your temple.

According to your name, O God, so also is your praise at the ends of the earth; your right hand is full of righteousness.

Let mount Zion rejoice, let the daughters of Judah leap joyfully on account of your judgments, O Lord.

For this is God our God into the coming age and into age of age; he himself will shepherd us into the ages.[131]

Third Day – 8th Hour

O God, liberate me in your name and judge me in your power.

Listen closely to my prayer, O God, give ear to the utterances of my mouth.

For strangers arose against me, and mighty

ones sought my soul; they did not set God before them.

For behold, God rescues me! and the Master is my soul's helper.

He will divert the evil things to my enemies. O destroy completely them in your truth!

Willingly I shall sacrifice unto you, O LORD, I will sing praise to your name, for it is good;

For you delivered me out of every affliction, and my eye observed it among my enemies. [132]

We have this treasure in jars of clay, so that the supremacy of the power would be from God and not from us,

Being squeezed in everything but not crushed, being perplexed but not completely perplexed,

Being persecuted but not abandoned, being thrown down but not destroyed,

Always carrying around the death of the Master Jesus in the body, in order that the life of Jesus would also be seen in our body.

For we the living are always handed over into death on account of Jesus, so that the life of Jesus would be seen in our dying body. [133]

Listen closely to my pleading, O God, attend to my prayer!

In the exhaustion of my heart, I cried out to
you from the ends of the earth; you uplifted me
in the rock.

You led me, for you became my hope, a strong
tower from the enemy's face.

Into the ages will I sojourn in your tabernacle; I
will be sheltered in the shelter of your wings.

For you, O God, listened closely to my vows;
you gave an inheritance to those who fear your
name.

You will add days upon the king's days; his
years will be until the days of a generation and
a generation.

He will remain before God into the coming age.
who will seek out his lovingkindness and truth?

Into age of age, I will strum to your name in
this way, to render my vows day after day.[134]

Master, toward whom shall we go? you have
the utterances of timeless life;

And we have trusted and known that you are
the Anointed King the Son of the living God.[135]

Third Day – 9th Hour

Do not rebuke me in your wrath, O Lord, nor
discipline me in your anger.

For your arrows were implanted in me, and

your hand pressed firmly upon me;

From the face of your anger, there is no healing in my flesh; from the face of my sin, there is no peace in my bones.

For my lawless deeds rose over my head; they were weighed upon me as a heavy burden.

My wounds stank and decayed from the face of my foolishness.

I suffered hardship, and I was entirely bent down; sulking was I going the whole day.

For my hips were filled of mockings, and healing is not in my flesh;

Severely was I harmed and humbled, I was howling from the groaning of my heart.

Before you is all my desire, O Lord, and my groaning is not concealed from you.

My heart was troubled, my strength abandoned me; and the light of my eyes, even it is not with me.

My friends and my neighbors came near, and opposite from me did they stand; even my nearest relatives stood from afar;

And those who seek my soul did violence; and the ones who seek evils for me spoke futilities, and they contemplated deceptions the whole day.

Yet I was not hearing—like a deaf man and like

a speechless man who opens not his mouth—

And I became like a person who does not hear and does not have rebuttals in his mouth.

For I expected upon you, Lord; you will listen closely, O Lord my God.

For I said, Never should my enemies rejoice over me; and they boasted before me when my feet were shaken.

For I am ready for the whips, and my grief is continually before me.

For I will report my lawlessness and show care over my sin.

Yet my enemies live and have prevailed over me, and they were multiplied who hate me unjustly;

Those who repay evil things for good were slandering me, because I was following after righteousness; and they discarded me, the beloved like a detested dead man.

Do not abandon me, Lord; O my God, you would not depart from me;

O Lord of my liberation, attend to my rescue![136]

Third Day – Intercession Hour

You who briefly suffer, may the God of all generosity who calls you into his timeless glory in Anointed King Jesus, may he equip, stabilize, strengthen, and ground you.

To him be glory and power into the ages of ages, amen![137]

From the day we heard, we do not stop praying on your behalf and requesting that you would be filled with the recognition of his will in all wisdom and spiritual comprehension,

For you to walk worthily of the Master into every effort to please, bringing forth fruit in every good work and growing into the recognition of God,

Being empowered in all power according to the might of his glory into all endurance and long-suffering with gladness,

Thanking the Father who enables us for the sharing of the inheritance of the saints in light,

Who rushed us out of the authority of darkness and transferred us into the kingdom of his beloved Son,

In whom we have the ransom payment, the release of sins;

Who is the icon of the invisible God, the firstborn of all creation,

Because all things visible and invisible were created by him in heaven and on earth, whether thrones or lordships, whether rulers or authorities, all things were created through him and for him,

And he is before all things, and all things have taken shape in him,

And he is the head of the body, the congregation; he who is the beginning, the firstborn out of the dead, in order that he would become foremost in all things

Because all the fullness was pleased to dwell in him

And through him to fully change all things for him, making peace through the blood of his cross; all things through him, whether things on earth or in the heavens.[138]

May the LORD hear you in the day of affliction; may the name of the God of Jacob shield you.

May he dispatch aid to you from the sanctuary; and out of Zion, may he assist you.

May he be mindful of your every sacrifice and cherish your whole burnt offering.

May he give to you according to your heart and fulfill your every intention.

We will rejoice in your rescue, and we will boast in the name of our God; may the LORD fulfill all your requests.

Now I knew that the LORD saved his anointed

one; he will heed him from his holy heaven; the liberation of his right hand is in his sovereignty.

They boast in chariots, and others in horses; yet we will boast the name of the LORD our God.

They were footbound and fell, yet we rose again and were set upright.

O LORD, save your king and heed us in the day we call upon you.[139]

May the God of endurance and encouragement grant to you to contemplate the same thing with one another according to Anointed King Jesus,

So that with one heart you would glorify in one mouth the God and Father of our Master, Anointed King Jesus.

May the God of anticipation cram you of all joy and peace while trusting, in order for you to abound in anticipation in the Holy Spirit's power.[140]

Third Day – 11th Hour

O my God, take me away from my enemies, and ransom me from those who rise up against me.

Rush me away from those who work lawlessness, and save me from men of blood.

For lo, they hunted my soul; mighty ones set upon me; rebellion is neither mine nor is sin mine, O LORD.

I ran without rebellion, and they kept straight on; O awaken fully into my controversy, and see!

O my strength, I will look toward you, because God is my helper.

Yet at dawn I will sing to your power and celebrate your lovingkindness, for you became my helper and refuge in the day of my affliction.

O my rescuer, I strum to you; for you are my assistance and my aid, O God my God.[141]

Even until the present hour we hunger and thirst and go naked and roam and are beaten;

And we tire, working with our own hands; being insulted, we bless; being persecuted, we endure, being despised, we encourage;

We were made to become like the abhorrences of the world, the scum of all things until the present time.[142]

Will my soul not be submitted unto God? for my liberation comes from him;

For he himself is my God and my liberator, my

helper; I could not be greatly shaken.

How long will you assault a person? you all murder, as on a slanted wall and a pushed fence.

But they plotted to drive away my honor; they ran in falsehood; they were blessing in their mouth, and they were cursing in their heart.

O my soul, be submitted nevertheless unto God; for my endurance comes from him.

For he himself is my God and my liberator, my helper; never shall I flee.

My liberation and my glory are with God. O God of my rescue, my expectation is also upon God.

All the gathering of the people, expect upon him; pour out your hearts before him! God is our rescuer.

But futile are the children of men; the children of men are false with the scales, to do injustice; they are from futility altogether.

Once did God speak, twice I heard these things,

That the power is from God; and yours, O Lord, is the rescue, for you yourself repay to each one according unto his works.[143]

Third Day – 12th Hour

O God, you drove us away and took us down;

you were angered, and you pitied us.

You shook the land and disturbed it; O heal its fractures, for it was rocked.

You showed harshness to your people; make us drink from the wine of conviction!

To those who fear you, you gave a sign to flee from the face of the bow.

So that those who love you would be delivered, O save by your right hand and heed me!

Are you not, O God, the one who drives us away? and will you not come out, O God, among our forces?

Give rescue to us from affliction; for the safety of man is futile.[144]

Holy, holy, holy is the Lord God the Omnipotence, who was and is and is coming.

Let there be glory and honor and gratitude to the one sitting upon the throne, he who lives into the ages of ages,

Worthy are you the Holy One, our Master and God, to take the glory and the honor and the the power; for you created all things, and they existed and were created because of your will![145]

O God my God, early I will rise toward you; my

soul thirsted for you. how often did my flesh thirst for you in a desolate and untrodden and waterless land?

This way I appeared before you in the sanctuary, to see your power and your glory.

My lips will praise you, for your lovingkindness is better than many lives.

This way I will bless you in my life, I will lift up my hands in your name.

O that my soul would be crammed full, as if from fat and oil; and my mouth will praise, as the lips of rejoicing.

If I was mindful of you upon my blanket, I was pondering you in the morning hours;

And I will leap joyfully in the shelter of your wings, for you became my rescuer.

My soul clung to following you; your right hand assisted me.

Yet in vain did they themselves seek my soul; they will enter into the lowest parts of the ground;

They will be delivered into hands of swords, they will be dinners for foxes.

Yet the king will rejoice before God; everyone swearing by him will be praised, for the mouth of those who speak unjust things will be gagged.[146]

Midweek Day – 1st Hour

Awake O sleeper and arise from the dead, and the Anointed King will shine upon you.[147]

Blessed be the God and Father of our Master Anointed King Jesus, the one regenerating us according to his powerful rescue into a living expectation through the resurrection of Anointed King Jesus from the dead;

As many as were baptized into Anointed King Jesus, we were baptized into his death

In the Name of the Father and of the Son and the Holy Spirit

The Encourager,

The Comforter,

The Exhorter, the Spirit of truth who proceeds from the Father

And he will convict the world about sin and righteousness and judgment.

Whenever someone would turn toward the Lord, the veil is lifted.

The Lord is the Spirit; yet where the Spirit of the Lord is, freedom is there.

We all with unveiled face, viewing the glory of the Lord as in a mirror, are being transformed into the same image from glory into glory, even as from the Lord the Spirit.

We rejoice in tribulations, having perceived that tribulation produces perseverance,

And perseverance proof, and proof hope,

And hope does not disappoint because God's love has been poured out in our hearts through the Holy Spirit who has been given to us.

For these are God's children, as many as are led by God's Spirit

The Spirit of adoption, in whom we cry out, Daddy Father!

The same Spirit testifies together with our spirit that we are God's offspring.

If we are offspring, also heirs, heirs of God, and co-heirs of the Anointed King if indeed we co-suffer, in order that we would also be co-glorified.

And likewise the Spirit assists in our weaknesses; for we have not perceived what we should necessarily pray about, but the same Spirit super-intercedes on our behalf in unutterable groanings[148]

O for the LORD to liberate me! O God, hold attention to my rescue!

Let those who seek my soul be ashamed and embarrassed; let those who wish evils for me be turned backwards and be completely ashamed!

Let those who say to me, Well done well done, be immediately turned away, being ashamed!

Let all those who seek you leap joyfully and make merry before you; and let those who love your liberation always say, be magnified O God!

Yet I myself am poor and needy; rescue me, O God! You yourself are my rescuer and my deliverer; O LORD, you would not delay.[149]

Midweek Day – 2nd Hour

Every land, shout joyfully to God,

Indeed, strum unto his name, add glory to his praise!

Say to God, How formidable are your works! amid the plenitude of your power, your enemies will falsify you;

All the land will bow down to you and strum unto you; they must strum unto your name.

Come and behold the works of God! he is formidable in his counsels on behalf of the children of men,

The one who turns the sea into dry land; they will pass through on foot in a river. there they will rejoice before him

Who masters the age by his power; his eyes

oversee the nations; as for those who provoke, let them not be exalted in themselves!

O nations, bless our God, and make heard the sound of his praise,

He who places my soul into life and gives not my feet into trembling.

For you tested us, O God. you purged us, as the silver is smelted;

You brought us into the snare; you placed afflictions on our back.

You mounted people upon our heads; we passed through fire and water, and you brought us out into refreshment.

Into your house I will enter with burnt offerings, I will render unto you my vows

Which my lips uttered and my mouth spoke during my affliction;

I will offer to you fatted burnt sacrifices with incense and rams; I will render to you oxen with goats.

All ye who fear God, come and hear and recount as many things as he did for my soul!

I cried out to him with my mouth, and I exalted by my tongue, saying:

If injustice were being observed in my heart, let the Lord listen not!

Therefore God did listen to me; he attended to

the voice of my pleading.

Blessed be God, who did not remove my prayer and his lovingkindness from me.[150]

To the only wise God our liberator be glory and majesty, might and authority, even now and into all the ages; amen![151]

Midweek Day – 3rd Hour

Our Father in heaven, your name be hallowed,

Your kingdom come, and your will happen on earth as it does in heaven,

Give us today our daily bread,

And release for us our debts, as we ourselves also release our debtors;

And bring us not into testing, but rush us away from the evil one. for yours is the kingdom and the power and the glory into the ages; amen![152]

May God rescue us and bless us, may he manifest his face to us,

In order to know your path in the land, and your liberation among all nations!

Let the peoples sing praise to you, O God; let all peoples sing praise to you!

Let nations make merry and leap joyfully, for you will judge the peoples in uprightness and guide the nations in the land.

Let the peoples sing praise to you, O God; let all peoples sing praise to you!

The land gave its fruit; O may God our God bless us!

May God bless us; and let all the ends of the earth be in awe of him![153]

O the depth of God's wealth and wisdom and knowledge! how unsearchable are his decisions and untraceable his paths!

For who knew the mind of the Lord? or who became his advisor?

Or who gave first to him and will be repaid by him?

Because all things are from him and through him and for him. to him be the glory into the ages; amen![154]

Midweek Day – 4th Hour

How good you are to Israel, O God, to those who are upright in heart.

Yet my feet were shaken a little, and slightly did my footsteps slip away.

For I, observing the peace of sinners, envied the lawless ones.

Behold, these are sinners, and they prosper;

they obtained wealth for the age.

And I said, Therefore in futility have I justified my heart and washed my hands in innocence;

And the whole day I became like one having been flogged, even into the early mornings was my conviction.

I was saying, This way I will explain it; behold, I've broken covenant with the lineage of your children.

And I undertook to know this; in front of me is weariness

Until I would enter into the sanctuary of God and comprehend their ends.

Yet you appointed unto them on account of their deceits, you cast them down when they were uplifted.

How suddenly they became for a desolation, they fainted and perished on account of their lawlessness.

Like a dream when awaking, O Lord, you will despise their image in your city.

For my heart was inflamed, and my inmost parts were changed,

And I, being despised and unknowing, became beastlike with you.

And I was with you through everything; you grasped my right hand,

You guided me in your counsel and received me with glory!

For what belongs to me in heaven, and what did I desire from you upon the earth?

My heart fainted, and my flesh; O God, you are the God of my heart, and my portion into the coming age.

For behold, those who distance themselves from you will perish; you completely destroyed everyone who prostitutes himself away from you.

Yet it is good for me to be cleaved unto God, to place my hope in the LORD so that I would proclaim all of your praises in the gates of the daughter of Zion.[155]

To the One who loves us and washes us from our sins in his blood, Anointed King Jesus, the trustworthy witness, the first born from the dead, and the Ruler of the kings of the earth.

Into ages of ages, let the glory and the power be unto him who made us a kingdom, as ministers unto his God and Father; amen.[156]

Midweek Day – 5th Hour

O God, why did you completely shove away, and why was your passion enraged at the sheep of your pasture?

Be mindful of your congregation which you obtained from the beginning; you ransomed the scepter of your inheritance, this mount Zion in which you encamped.

Uplift your hands completely at their arrogant deeds, at the many things which the enemy worked maliciously among your holy ones.

Those who hate you also boasted in the midst of your festival; they appointed their own signs as signs, and they did not know.

They burned your sanctuary in fire, they stomped the tabernacle of your name into the ground.

Together their kindred said in their heart: Come, and we should burn down all the festivals of God away from the earth!

How long, O God, shall the enemy reproach? does the opposing one not provoke your name completely?

Why do you completely turn away your hand, even your right hand from the midst of your bosom?

Yet God was our King from before the ages, he worked salvation in the midst of the land.

You took hold of the sea in your power; you crushed the heads of the dragons upon the water.

You yourself shattered the heads of the dragon, you gave him to the Ethiopians as meat.

You burst through the fountains and brooks; you dried up the rivers of the mighty.

Yours is the day, and yours is the night, you yourself created illumination and the sun.

You made all the mountains of the land; summer and spring, you yourself formed them.

Be mindful of this, that a hostile one insulted the LORD, and a foolish people provoked your name!

You would not deliver to the beasts a soul confessing unto you; you would not forget the souls of your needy ones.

Look closely into your covenant, for the darkened places of the land were crammed full of the houses of transgressions.

Let not the humbled one be turned away, having been shamed; a poor one and a needy one will praise your name.

Arise O God, judge your justice; be mindful of your insults by a fool the whole day.

You would not forget the voice of your petitioners; the arrogance of those who hate you arises before you continually.[157]

Holy, holy, holy is the Lord God the Omnipotence, who was and is and is coming.

Worthy are you the Holy One, our Master and God, to take the glory and the honor and the the power; for you created all things, and they existed and were created because of your will![158]

Midweek Day – 6th Hour

In Judea God is known, his name is great in Israel.

And his place became in peace, and his abode in Zion.

There he crushed the might of bows, armor and sword and war.

You illuminated marvelously from timeless mountains.

All the uncomprehending ones were disturbed in heart; they slept their sleep, and the men of wealth found nothing in their hands.

From your rebuke, O God of Jacob, those having mounted upon horses became drowsy.

You yourself are formidable, and who will stand in opposition to you? from that time came your anger.

Out of heaven you made a judgment heard; the land was frightened, and it was silenced in stillness

When God arose for judgment to liberate all the meek ones of the land.

For the contemplation of man will praise you, and the remainder of contemplation will celebrate you.

Make vows and render to the LORD your God! all those around him will bring gifts

To him who is formidable and who seizes the spirits of rulers, to him who is formidable to the kings of the land.[159]

Blessed be the God and Father of our Master Anointed King Jesus, the one who blesses us in every spiritual blessing among the heavenly places in the Anointed King,

Just as before the founding of the world he also favored us in him, in order for us to be holy and blameless before him in love,

Marking us in advance, according to the good pleasure of his desire, for adoption into him through Anointed King Jesus,

For the praise of the glory of his generosity with which he endowed us in the beloved one,

In whom we have the full ransom payment through his blood, the release from transgressions according to the wealth of his generosity,

From which he overflowed into us in all wisdom and thoughtfulness,

Making known to us the secret of his desire, according to his good pleasure, which he exhibited in him

For an administration of the filling up of the seasons, in order to reconstitute under one head in the Anointed King, all things on heaven and earth in him,

In whom we, being previously designated, were also allotted an inheritance according to an exhibition of the one who inwardly works all things according to the counsel of his desire,

So that we who have anticipated in the Anointed King would be for the praise of his glory[160]

Midweek Day – 7th Hour

Bless the LORD, O my soul; and everything within me, bless his holy name;

Bless the LORD, O my soul, and do not forget all his rewards;

He who shows mercy to all your lawless deeds, the one who heals all your diseases;

He who ransoms your life from decay; the one who crowns you in lovingkindness and pity;

The one who fills your desire with good things, for your youth to be renewed like that of an eagle.

The LORD is doing charitable deeds, and judgment for all those who are being harmed.

He made known his paths to Moses, his desires to the children of Israel.

The LORD is pitying and merciful, longsuffering and greatly merciful;

He will not be angered completely nor carry anger into the coming age;

He did not do to us according to our sins nor repay us according to our lawless deeds

For like the height of the sky from the ground, so the Lord empowered his lovingkindness toward those who fear him;

As much as the East extends from the West, so he distanced our transgressions away from us.

Just as a father pities his children,
the LORD pitied those who fear him,

For he himself knew our formation; be mindful that we are dust!

As for a human, his days are like grass; like a flower of the field, so he will flower forth;

For a breath passes through him, and it will not be and will no longer recognize its place.

Yet the lovingkindness of the LORD is from age

to age toward those who fear him, and his righteousness upon children's children

For those who guard his covenant and have been mindful of his commandments in order to do them.

The LORD prepared his throne in the heavens, and his kingdom overrules all.

Bless ye the LORD, all his angels, who are powerful in strength, doing his word in order to hear the sound of his words;

Bless ye the LORD, all his armies, his servants who do his desire;

Bless ye the LORD, all his works in every place of his dominion; bless the LORD, O my soul![161]

Midweek Day – 8th Hour

For these are God's children, as many as are led by God's Spirit,

The Spirit of adoption, in whom we cry out, Daddy Father!

The same Spirit testifies together with our spirit that we are God's offspring.

If we are offspring, also heirs, heirs of God, and co-heirs of the Anointed King if indeed we co-suffer, in order that we would also be co-glorified.

The longing of the creation anticipates the

unveiling of the children of God.

For we have perceived that all creation groans together and labors together until now.

Not only it, but even we ourselves having the first-fruits of the Spirit also groan in ourselves, anticipating an adoption, the full ransom of our body.

If we expect what we do not see, then we look forward through patience.

And likewise the Spirit assists in our weaknesses; for we have not perceived what we should necessarily pray about, but the same Spirit super-intercedes on our behalf in unutterable groanings[162]

O God, the nations came into your inheritance, they polluted your holy temple; they made Jerusalem into a garden-hut.

They placed the carcasses of your slaves as meat for the birds of the sky, the flesh of your saints for the beasts of the land;

They poured their blood around Jerusalem like water; and there was no one burying them.

We became a reproach to our neighbors, a derision and mockery to those around us.

How long, O LORD, will you be completely angered, and your jealousy be enflamed like fire?

Do not remember our ancient transgressions; let your compassions overtake us swiftly, for we were sorely impoverished.

Run to our cry, O God our liberator; deliver us for the sake of the glory of your name, O Lord, and be merciful toward our sins for your name's sake,

Lest the nations should say, Where is their God? and among the nations let the avenging of the outpoured blood of your slaves be made known before our eyes!

Let the groaning of the shackled ones enter before you; according to the greatness of your arm, preserve the children of those who have been slain.

We your people and the sheep of your pasture will give thanks to you into the coming age, we will proclaim your praise for generation and generation.[163]

Midweek Day – 9th Hour

Certainly I deem all things to be damage because of the superiority of the knowledge of my Master Anointed King Jesus, thanks to whom I have been damaged all things; and I deem them to be feces so that I would profit

And be found in him—not having my

righteousness from the law, but through trust of the Anointed King, having the righteousness from God which exists upon trust—

To know him and the power of his resurrection and the sharing of his sufferings, being conformed to his death[164]

Give attentiveness, you who shepherd Israel, the one guiding Joseph like sheep, the one sitting upon the cherubim, appear!

Before Ephraim and Benjamin and Manasseh, awaken your power and come and save us!

O God, return us and manifest your face; and we will be liberated.

O Lord God of armies, how long would you be angered against the prayer of your slave,

And feed us the bread of tears and have us drink from tears in measure?

You appointed us for a contradiction to our neighbors; even our enemies mocked us.

O Lord God of armies, return us and manifest your face, and we will be liberated.

You removed a vineyard from Egypt; you cast out nations, and you planted it;

You made a path before it and planted its roots, and the land was filled.

Its shadow covered hills, and its vines the

cedars of God;

It extended its branches as far as a sea, and its offshoots as far as the river.

Why did you tear down its fencing, and all those who go by the road stripped it?

A boar from the grove wasted it, and a lone wild beast devoured it.

O God of the armies, return us indeed, look upon us from heaven and behold and visit this vineyard

And restore it which your right hand planted, and look upon a son of man whom you empowered for yourself.

It was having been burned with fire and dug up; they will perish at the rebuke of your face.

Let your hand become upon the man of your right hand and upon a son of man whom you empowered for yourself.

And we could not depart from you; you will vivify us, and we will call upon your name.

O Lord God of armies, return us and manifest your face, and we will be liberated![165]

Midweek Day – Intercession Hour

Blessed are the poor, for the kingdom of God is yours.

Blessed are those who hunger now, for you will

be satisfied. blessed are those who sob now, for you will laugh.

Blessed are you whenever people would hate you and exclude you and insult you and reject your name as evil because of the son of man.

Rejoice and leap joyfully in that day, for your payment in heaven is much, for their fathers were doing the same things to the prophets.[166]

Teacher, I beg of you, look upon my son, for he is my only begotten son;

And behold, a spirit takes him, and suddenly it screams and convulses him with foam; and troublesomely it departs from him, crushing him.[167]

I lifted my eyes into the hills. from where does my rescue arrive?

My rescue is from the LORD who made the heaven and the earth.

He would not give your foot into shaking, nor would he lull the one who guards you.

Behold, he who guards Israel will neither tire nor slumber.

The LORD guards you, the LORD is your shelter at your right hand.

The sun will not enflame you by day, nor will

the moon enflame the night.

The LORD will guard you from every evil; he shall guard your soul.

The LORD will guard your entryway and your exit-way from now and until the age to come.[168]

For this reason I bend my knees unto the Father of our Master Anointed King Jesus,

From whom every paternal lineage is named in heaven and on earth,

So that according to the wealth of his glory he would grant unto you to be invigorated in power through his Spirit in the inner human,

In order for the Anointed King to dwell in your hearts through trust,

Having been rooted and founded in love so that you would fully prevail, to grasp with all the saints what is the width and length and depth and height of this love,

And to know the love of the Anointed King which goes beyond knowledge, in order that you would be filled into all the fullness of God.[169]

You who briefly suffer, may the God of all generosity who calls you into his timeless glory in Anointed King Jesus, may he equip, stabilize, strengthen, and ground you.

To him be glory and power into the ages of ages, amen![170]

Midweek Day – 11th Hour

Blessed are the poor in spirit, for theirs is the kingdom of the heavens.

Blessed are those who grieve, for they shall be encouraged.

Blessed are the meek, for they will inherit the land.

Blessed are those who hunger and thirst for righteousness, for they shall be satisfied.

Blessed are those who rescue, for they will be rescued.

Blessed are the clean in heart, for they will see God.

Blessed are those who make peace, for they shall be called God's children.

Blessed those having been persecuted because of righteousness, for theirs is the kingdom of the heavens.[171]

You were well pleased with your land, O Lord, you turned away the captivity of Jacob;
You released the transgressions for your

people, you covered all their sins.

You put to rest all your anger; you turned away from the anger of your heart.

Return us, O God of our deliverances, and turn away your wrath from us.

Will you be angered at us into the coming age or extend your anger from generation to generation?

O God, returning you will enliven us, and your people will rejoice before you.

Show your lovingkindness to us, O LORD, and give to us your deliverance.

I will hear what the LORD God will speak in me, for he will speak peace upon his people and upon his holy ones and upon those who turn their heart back toward him.

And his deliverance is near those who fear him, in order for glory to encamp in our land.

Compassion and truth met together; righteousness and peace deeply kissed;

Truth rose up out of the ground, and righteousness stooped down out of heaven.

Indeed the LORD will give kindness, and our land will give its crop;

Righteousness will go before him and will appoint his footsteps for a pathway.[172]

Midweek Day – 12th Hour

Great and marvelous are your works, Lord God Omnipotence. righteous and true are your paths, O King of the nations.

Lord, who could not fear and glorify your name? for you alone are pure, for all the nations will arrive and bow down before you, for your decrees were made visible.[173]

I will exalt you, O LORD; for you uplifted me and did not gladden my enemies over me.

O LORD my God, I cried out unto you, and you healed me;

You, LORD, brought up my soul out of hades; you liberated me from those who descend into a pit.

Strum to the LORD, O his holy ones, and give thanks in the mindfulness of his holiness;

For there is anger in his passion, and life in his desire; weeping will encamp in the evening, and rejoicing will encamp into the morning.

Yet I said in my prosperity: Into the coming age I could not be shaken.

LORD, in your will you provided power for my beauty; yet you turned away your face, and I became disturbed.

To you, O LORD, I will cry out; and I will plead

unto God:

What profit is there in my blood, when I descend into decay? will dust acknowledge you or announce your truth?

The LORD heard and aided me, the LORD became my rescuer.

You turned for me my mourning into dancing, you ripped through my sackcloth and wrapped me with gladness,

So that my glory would strum unto you, and I could not be grieved; O LORD my God, into the coming age I will give thanks unto you![174]

O God, Lord of my liberation, I cried out before you by day and by night;

Let my prayer enter in your sight; incline your ear into my pleading, O Lord!

For my soul was filled from harmful things, and my life approached toward hades;

I was accounted with those who descend into the pit. I became like an incurable person set free among the dead,

Like wounded men in a coma having been tossed in a grave, whom you remembered no longer, and they were thrust out away from your hand.

They put me in the lowest pit, among dark

things and death's shadow.

My eyes weakened from poverty; the whole day I cried out toward you, LORD, I spread out my hands toward you

And I cried out before you, O LORD; and early in the morning my prayer shall anticipate you![175]

Fifth Day – 1st Hour

Awake O sleeper and arise from the dead, and the Anointed King will shine upon you.[176]

O Lord, you became a refuge for us in generation and generation;

Before the mountains came into existence and the land and the inhabitation were formed, even from age until age, you are.

You would not turn away humanity into debasement; and you said, Children of men, turn back!

For a thousand years in your eyes are like the day, yesterday which passed, and like a watch in the night.

Years will be their displeasures. in the morning, may the day pass away like grass,

In the morning, may it bloom and pass away; in the evening, O may it fall away, may it be hardened and withered.

For we fainted amid your anger, and in your passion we were troubled.

You placed our transgressions before you; our lifetime was in the light of your face.

For all our days ended, we expired amid your passion; our years were esteemed like a spiderweb.

As for the days of our years, in them are seventy years; yet even if they happen in great strengths, there are eighty years, and most of them are hardship and toil; for meekness came upon us, and we will be chastened.

Who knows the power of your anger and your passion from the fear of you?

So make known your right hand to number them in wisdom, and the things which have been bound up in the heart.

How long will it be? return, O LORD, and be implored on behalf of your slaves!

In the early morning we were filled of your compassion, and we leapt joyfully and made merry amid all our days;

We became happy in exchange for the days when you humbled us, the years when we saw harmful things.

Look at your slaves and your works, and guide their children,

And let the splendor of the LORD our God be upon us; and prosper the works of our hands for us.[177]

If the LORD would not construct the house, those who construct it toil for futility. if the LORD would not guard the city, the watchman stays awake for uselessness.[178]

Holy, holy, holy is the Lord God the Omnipotence, who was and is and is coming.

Let there be glory and honor and gratitude to the one sitting upon the throne, he who lives into the ages of ages,

Worthy are you the Holy One, our Master and God, to take the glory and the honor and the the power; for you created all things, and they existed and were created because of your will![179]

Fifth Day – 2nd Hour

Glory to God in highest places and peace upon earth, goodwill among people![180]

Even until the present hour we hunger and thirst and go naked and roam and are beaten;

And we tire, working with our own hands; being insulted, we bless; being persecuted, we endure, being despised, we encourage;

We were made to become like the abhorrences of the world, the scum of all things until the present time.[181]

Incline your ear and hear me, O LORD, for I am poor and needy.

Guard my soul, for I am holy; O my God deliver your slave who expects upon you.

Rescue me, O Lord, for I will cry out unto you the whole day!

Gladden the soul of your slave, O Lord, for I lifted my soul unto you.

Because you, O Lord, are kind and tolerant and greatly compassionate to all those who call upon you.

Give ear to my prayer, O Lord, and heed the sound of my pleading.

In the day of my affliction I cried out to you, because you listened closely to me.

There is none like you among the gods, O Lord, and there are no works corresponding to yours.

As many nations as you made, O Lord, they will all come near and bow down before you and glorify your name,

Because you, great are you and doing marvelous things; you are the only great God.

Guide me in your path, O Lord, and I will proceed in your truth; let my heart rejoice to fear your name.

O Lord my God, in my whole heart I will sing praise to you and glorify your name into the coming age,

Because your compassion for me is great, and

you rushed my soul out of the lowest hades.

O God, the lawless ones arose against me, and an assembly of mighty ones sought after my soul, and they did not put you before them.

You, O Lord God, are pitying and compassionate, longsuffering and greatly compassionate and truthful.

Look upon me and rescue me; give your strength to your servant and liberate the child of your maidservant.

Make a sign with me for good, and let those who hate me see it and be turned away in shame. for you, O LORD, rescued me and comforted me.[182]

To the only wise God our liberator be glory and majesty, might and authority, even now and into all the ages; amen![183]

Fifth Day – 3rd Hour

There is one body and one Spirit, even as you were called in one hope of your calling,

One Master, one faith, one baptism,

One God and Father of all, who is upon all and through all and within us all.[184]

Master, if you would desire, you are able to cleanse me.

Master Jesus, rescue us!

Jesus, Son of David, rescue me. Son of David, rescue me![185]

The one who dwells in the aid of the most High will encamp in the shadow of the God of heaven.

I will say to the LORD, You are my overshielder and my haven, O my God; I shall expect upon him,

For he himself will rush me out of the snare of hunters and away from an agitating word.

He will overshadow you by the width of his back, and you will hope beneath his wings; his truth will encircle you in armor.

You will not be frightened from nocturnal terror, or from the arrow flying in daytime,

From a deed which passes through in darkness, or from a mishap and demon at noon.

A thousand will fall away from your side, and ten thousand from your right hand, yet it will not approach toward you;

But with your eyes you will notice, and you will see the reward of sinners.

For you, O LORD, are my expectation; you appointed the most High as your refuge.

Evil things will not come forth before you, and

a scourge will not come near to your tent,

For he will command his angels concerning you, to guard you in all your paths;

They will lift you upon hands, lest you should strike your foot against a stone;

You will tread upon an asp and viper and trample down a lion and serpent.

Because he hoped upon me, I will also rescue him; I will shelter him, because he knew my name.

He will call upon me, and I will listen closely to him; I am with him in affliction, and I will lift away and glorify him.

I will fill him with length of days and show to him my liberation.[186]

Fifth Day – 4th Hour

Therefore I implore first of all for pleadings, prayers, intercessions, and thanks to be made on behalf of all people,

On behalf of kings and all those being in high position, so that we would lead a quiet and unshakable life in all devotedness and respectability.

For this is beautiful and fully acceptable in the sight of God our Liberator,

Who wants all people to be liberated and to

come into the recognition of truth.[187]

You heard that it was uttered: You shall love your neighbor and hate your enemies.

Yet I myself say to you, Love your enemies; bless those who curse you; do well to those who hate you, and pray on behalf of those who threaten you and persecute you,

So that you would become children of your Father in the heavens; for his sun rises upon evil people and good ones, and it rains upon the righteous and the unrighteous.

For if you would love those who love you, what reward do you have? do the tax collectors not do the same?

And if you would only embrace your friends, what generosity do you perform? do the tax collectors not also do so?

Therefore you shall be complete, just as your Father in the heavens is complete.[188]

O God, who will be compared to you? You should not be silent nor pacify, O God;

For behold, your enemies roared, and those who hate you lifted their head,

They wickedly devised a plan toward your people, and they plotted against your holy ones.

Fill their faces with dishonor, and they will seek your name, O LORD.

They should know that your name is the LORD; you alone are most High over all the earth.[189]

The LORD reigned, he was clothed with majesty; the LORD was clothed with strength and girded himself; and indeed he solidified the world which will not be shaken.

From that time, your throne was ready; from eternity you are you.

O LORD, the rivers lifted up, the rivers lifted up their voices;

With the voices of many waters, marvelous are the waves of the sea; marvelous in the heights is the LORD.

Your testimonies were trusted precisely; O LORD, holiness suits your house for length of days.[190]

As many as were immersed in the Anointed King have put on the Anointed King.[191]

Into ages of ages, let honor and glory be unto the King of the ages, the incorruptible, unseen, only wise God; amen![192]

Fifth Day – 5th Hour

Blessed be the God and Father of our Master Anointed King Jesus, the one regenerating us according to his powerful rescue into a living expectation through the resurrection of Anointed King Jesus from the dead;

As many as were baptized into Anointed King Jesus, we were baptized into his death

In the Name of the Father and of the Son and the Holy Spirit

The Encourager,

The Comforter,

The Exhorter, the Spirit of truth who proceeds from the Father

And he will convict the world about sin and righteousness and judgment.

The Lord is the Spirit; yet where the Spirit of the Lord is, freedom is there.

For these are God's children, as many as are led by God's Spirit

The Spirit of adoption, in whom we cry out, Daddy Father!

The same Spirit testifies together with our spirit that we are God's offspring.

If we are offspring, also heirs, heirs of God, and co-heirs of the Anointed King if indeed we co-suffer, in order that we would also be co-glorified.

And likewise the Spirit assists in our weaknesses; for we have not perceived what we should necessarily pray about, but the same Spirit super-intercedes on our behalf in unutterable groanings[193]

O Lord, I cried out unto you, hear me; heed the voice of my pleading when I have cried out unto you.

Let my prayer be guided before you as incense, and the lifting up of my hands be an evening sacrifice.

Set a watch, O Lord, before my mouth and a door of containment about my lips.

Incline not my heart into evil words, to plead excuses in sins with people who work lawlessness, and I could not collude with their favorite things.

A righteous one will chasten me and rebuke me in lovingkindness; yet the olive oil of a sinner must not moisten my head. for even amid their goodwill, my prayer shall continually be.

Their judges were swallowed down near a rock; they will hear my statements because they were seasoned.

As a clump of earth was broken upon the earth, so our bones were scattered beside hades.

For my eyes are toward you, Lord GOD; I expected upon you, do not discard my soul.

O guard me from the trap which they introduced to me, and from the snares of those who work lawlessness.

Sinners will fall into his dragnet; alone am I until I would get past it.[194]

To the only wise God our liberator be glory and majesty, might and authority, even now and into all the ages; amen![195]

Fifth Day – 6th Hour

Come, we would rejoice in the LORD, we would shout joyfully unto God our liberator;

We should come before his face with thanksgiving, and with psalms we should shout joyfully unto him!

For the LORD is a great God, and a great king over all the gods;

For in his hand are the extremities of the land, and his are the heights of the mountains;

For his is the sea, and he made it, and his hands formed the dry land.

Come, we should bow down and fall down

before him, and we should weep in front of the LORD who made us;

For he himself is our God, and we are the people of his pasture, and sheep of his hand. today if you would hear his voice,

You should not harden your hearts as in the provocation, according to the day of testing in the wilderness,

Where your fathers tested me; they proved and saw my works.

Forty years was I angered by that generation and said, Always they are misled in the heart, and they knew not my paths;

As I swore in my anger: If they will enter into my rest![196]

As many as were baptized into Anointed King Jesus, we were baptized into his death.

Therefore we were buried together with him through baptism into death; so that just as the Anointed King was roused from the dead ones through the Father's glory, in this way we too should walk in novelty of life.

For if we have become planted together in the likeness of his death, yet also of the resurrection will we be,

Knowing this, that our old person was crucified

together, in order that the body of sin would be shut down, for us to no longer a slave to sin;

For the one who dies has been made righteous away from sin.

If we died together in the Anointed King, we trust that we will also live together in him,

Having perceived that the Anointed King, being awakened out of the dead, no longer dies; death no longer masters him.

For which death he died, he died once only unto sin; yet which life he lives, he lives unto God.[197]

The LORD reigned; let the earth leap joyfully, the many islands gladden!

Zion heard and gladdened, and the daughters of Judea leapt joyfully because of your judgments, O LORD;

For you are the LORD most High over all the land; you were exalted above all the gods.[198]

Fifth Day – 7th Hour

As confessed, great is the mystery of the faith; God was manifested in the flesh, justified in the Spirit, seen by angels, proclaimed in the nations, trusted in the world, and taken up in glory.[199]

Sing ye a new song unto the LORD; let all the earth sing unto the LORD;

Sing to the LORD, bless his name, proclaim the gospel of his liberation day after day;

Report his glory among the nations, and his marvelous deeds among all the peoples!

For great is the LORD and greatly praiseworthy; formidable is he over all the gods;

For all the gods of the nations are demons, yet the LORD made the heavens;

Thanksgiving and beauty are before him, holiness and magnificence are in his sanctuary.

Bring to the LORD, O tribes of the nations, bring glory and honor to the LORD.

Bring to the LORD glory unto his name, take sacrifices and go into his courts;

Bow down to the LORD in his holy court; let all the ground be shaken from his face!

Say among the nations, The LORD reigned, and indeed he established the world which will not be shaken, he will judge the peoples uprightly.

Let the heavens be glad, and the land exult; let the sea be shaken, and the fullness thereof!

The plains and all things in them will rejoice, then all the trees of the wood will leap joyfully

Before the face of the LORD, because he comes, for he comes to judge the earth; he will judge the inhabitation in righteousness, and the peoples in his truth.[200]

We give thanks to you, Lord God the Omnipotence who was and is and is coming, for you have taken your great power and reigned[201]

Worthy are you to take the scroll and to open up its seals, for you were butchered, and with your blood you purchased us unto God out of every tribe and tongue and people and nation,

And you made them kings and ministers to our God; and they will reign upon the earth.

Worthy is the little Lamb, the one having been butchered, to get the power and the fullness and wisdom and strength and honor and glory and blessing.

To the One sitting upon the throne and to the little Lamb be the blessing and the honor and the glory and the might into the ages of ages![202]

Yes, amen; come, Lord Jesus!

May the generosity of the Master Anointed King Jesus be with all the saints; amen![203]

Fifth Day – 8th Hour

When the hour had come, he reclined, and his twelve apostles with him.

And he said to them, With longing, I have longed to eat this passover with you before I am to suffer."[204]

How beloved are your dwellings, O LORD of armies.

My soul longs and faints for the courts of the LORD; my heart and my flesh leapt joyfully in the living God.

Indeed, even a sparrow found a house for itself, and a turtledove a nest for herself where she may lay her young, your altars, O LORD of armies, my King and my God.

Blessed are those who dwell in your house, they will praise you into ages of ages.

Blessed is the man whose help is from you, O Lord; he made a covenant in his heart to go up

In the valley of weeping into a place which he covenanted; and the lawgiver will indeed grant blessings.

They will proceed from strength to strength; the God of gods will be seen in Zion.

O LORD God of armies, listen closely to my prayer; give ear, O God of Jacob!

O God our overshielder, behold and look upon the face of your anointed.

For one day in your courts is better than thousands outside; I preferred to be thrown away in the house of my God rather than to dwell in the tabernacles of sinners.

For the Lord God loves compassion and truth, he will give favor and glory; the Lord shall not withhold good things for those who proceed in innocence.

O Lord of armies, blessed is the man who expects upon you![205]

Sing to the Lord a new song, for he did marvelous things; his right hand and his holy arm liberated for himself!

The Lord made known his liberation, he unveiled his righteousness in the sight of the nations.

Let him remember his lovingkindness for Jacob, and his truth for the house of Israel; all the ends of the earth saw the liberation of our God.

Shout joyfully unto the Lord, all the earth, sing and rejoice and strum!

Strum unto the Lord with a harp, with a harp and the sound of strumming;

With metal trumpets and the sound of a

trumpet made from horns, make a joyful noise before the LORD, the King!

Let the sea be shaken and its fullness, the inhabited world and those who dwell in it;

The rivers will clap their hands, the hills will leap joyfully,

For he will arrive to judge the land; he will judge the world in righteousness, and the peoples in uprightness.[206]

Fifth Day – Intercession Hour

I do not ask that you would take them out of the world, but that you would guard them from the evil one.

Hallow them in your truth. your word is truth.[207]

Father, forgive them; for they know not what they do.[208]

May the God of endurance and encouragement grant to you to contemplate the same thing with one another according to Anointed King Jesus,

So that with one heart you would glorify in one mouth the God and Father of our Master, Anointed King Jesus.

May the God of anticipation cram you of all joy

and peace while trusting, for you to abound in anticipation in the Holy Spirit's power.[209]

May the LORD hear you in the day of affliction; may the name of the God of Jacob shield you.

May he dispatch aid to you from the sanctuary; and out of Zion, may he assist you.

May he be mindful of your every sacrifice and cherish your whole burnt offering.

May he give to you according to your heart and fulfill your every intention.

We will rejoice in your deliverance, and we will boast in the name of our God; may the LORD fulfill all your requests.

Now I knew that the LORD saved his anointed one; he will heed him from his holy heaven; the liberation of his right hand is in his sovereignty.

They boast in chariots, and others in horses; yet we will boast the name of the LORD our God.

They were footbound and fell, yet we rose again and were set upright.

O LORD, save your king and heed us in the day we call upon you.[210]

Blessed are the poor, for the kingdom of God is yours.

Blessed are those who hunger now, for you will

be satisfied. blessed are those who sob now, for you will laugh.

Blessed are you whenever people would hate you and exclude you and insult you and reject your name as evil because of the son of man.

Rejoice and leap joyfully in that day, for your payment in heaven is much, for their fathers were doing the same things to the prophets.[211]

The Lord bless you and keep you,

The Lord make his face to shine upon you and be merciful to you,

The Lord lift up his face upon you and give you peace.[212]

Fifth Day – 10th Hour

But behold, the hand of the one betraying me is upon the table.[213]

Come to my aid, O God, for a man trampled me down; he afflicted me, fighting the whole day.

My enemies trampled me down the whole day, for many are those who battle me from on high.

Daily I will be frightened, yet I will expect upon you.

In God I will recommend my words the whole day. I expected upon God, I will not be frightened; what will flesh do to me?

The whole day they were detesting my words; all of their calculations for evil are against me.

They will dwell as strangers and hide away, they will watch my heel just as they awaited my soul.

On no account will you make them safe, O God, you will bring down the peoples in anger.

I proclaimed my life to you; you placed my tears before you, as it is in your promise also.

My enemies will turn back to the things behind in whichever day I would call upon you; behold, I knew that you are my God!

Unto God I will praise his utterance; unto the LORD I will praise his word.

I expected upon God, I will not be afraid; what will a human do to me?

O God, in me are the vows which I will render to you in praise,

For you delivered my soul from death and my feet from sliding, in order to be pleasing before God in the light of the living ones.[214]

It is the LORD who reigned and who sits upon the cherubim, so let the peoples be angered and the land be shaken!

The LORD is great in Zion, and high over all the peoples.

Let them sing praise to your great name, for it is fearful and holy.

A king's honor also loves judgment; it was you who prepared uprightness, it was you who made judgment and righteousness in Jacob.

Uplift the LORD our God and bow down at the footstool of his feet, for he is holy!

Moses and Aaron are among his priests, and Samuel among those who call upon his name; they were calling upon the LORD, and he heeded them,

He was speaking before them in a pillar of cloud; they were guarding his testimonies and his ordinances which he gave to them.

O LORD our God, you were heeding them; O God, you were becoming merciful to them, even when you were making vengeance against all their habits.

Lift up the LORD our God, and bow down at his holy hill! because the LORD our God is holy.[215]

Fifth Day – 11th Hour

According to habit, he went into the mount of olives, and his disciples accompanied him. Arriving at the place, he said to them, Pray you would not enter into temptation.[216]

With my voice I cried out before the Lord; with my voice I was before God, and he heeded me.

In the day of my affliction I sought after God; I was before him with my hands at night, and I was not deceived; my soul refused to be comforted.

I was mindful of God, and I gladdened; I pondered, and my spirit declined.

My eyes anticipated the night watches; I was troubled and did not speak.

I considered the olden days, I was mindful of eternal years, and I took concern;

At night I pondered with my heart, and my spirit was probing.

Will the LORD push me away and no longer be pleased into the ages?

Or will he cut off his lovingkindness from generation to generation?

Or will he forget to take pity, or will he constrain his pities in his anger?

And I said, Now I have begun; this change is from the right hand of the Most High.

I remembered the works of the LORD, for I will remember your wonders from the start

And I will meditate in all your works and

ponder in your habits.

O God, your path is in the holy place; who is a god great like our God?

You are the God who does wonders, making known your power among the peoples;

You ransomed by your arm your people, the children of Jacob and Joseph.

The waters saw you, O God; the waters saw you and were frightened, and the deeps were disturbed, a multitude of the noise of waters.

The clouds gave a sound, and indeed your arrows pass through them;

The sound of your thunder was in the circle, your lightnings shined in the world, the land was shaken and became tremorous.

Your path is in the sea, and your pathways in many waters, and your tracks will not be known.

You guided your people like sheep by the hand of Moses and Aaron.[217]

Fifth Day – 12th Hour

He returned and again found them sleeping; for their eyes were being heavy, and they had not known what to reply.[218]

Blessed is the one who considers a poor and

needy person; the Lord will deliver him in an evil day.

May the Lord guard him and vivify him and bless him in the land, and may he not deliver him into the hand of his enemy.

May the Lord rescue him on his couch of pain; during his infirmity you converted his bed into safety.

I said, O Lord rescue me; heal my soul, for I sinned against you!

My enemies spoke evil things against me: When will he die, and his name perish?

And if he was going inside to see me, he was speaking idly; his heart gathered lawlessness to himself; he was going outside and talking.

All my enemies were whispering together against me; against me they were devising evil things for me,

They laid down a lawless case against me: Surely the sleeping one will not set forth to rise again?

For even my man of peace whom I hoped upon, the one who eats my bread, he enlarged a trap before me;

O Lord, aid me and resurrect me, and I will repay to them.

By this I knew that you have delighted in me,

because my enemy could not rejoice over me.

Yet you assisted me because of innocence, and you established me before you into the coming age.

Blessed be the LORD God of Israel from age to age. amen, amen![219]

Master, if you would desire, you are able to cleanse me.

Master Jesus, rescue us!

Jesus, Son of David, rescue me! Son of David, rescue me![220]

When the LORD returned the captivity of Zion, we became as those who have been comforted.

Then our mouth was filled with gladness, and our tongue with rejoicing, then they will say among the nations: The LORD did great things with them!

Great things the LORD did with us; we became a people who revel.

O LORD, return our captivity like streams in the south.

Those who sow in tears will reap in exultation.

Leaving, they were going and sobbing, carrying their seeds; yet coming they will approach in jubilation, carrying their harvest bundles.[221]

Sixth Day – 1st Hour

Awake O sleeper and arise from the dead, and the Anointed King will shine upon you.[222]

Ready is my heart, O God, ready is my heart; I will sing and strum in my glory.

Be awakened, lyre and harp! early I shall be awakened.

I will sing praise to you among the peoples, O LORD, and I will strum to you among the nations,

For your lovingkindness is great above the skies, and your truth as far as the clouds.

O God, be exalted above the skies, and your glory over all the land!

So that your beloved ones would be delivered, liberate by your right hand, and hear from me!

Give to us a rescue from affliction; because the liberation by a human is futile.

In God we will work a miracle, and he himself will scorn our enemies.[223]

Blessed be the God and Father of our Master Anointed King Jesus, the one regenerating us according to his powerful rescue into a living expectation through the resurrection of Anointed King Jesus from the dead.

As many as were baptized into Anointed King Jesus, we were baptized into his death.

In the Name of the Father and of the Son and the Holy Spirit.

The Encourager,

The Comforter,

The Exhorter, the Spirit of truth who proceeds from the Father

And he will convict the world about sin and righteousness and judgment.

For these are God's children, as many as are led by God's Spirit

The Spirit of adoption, in whom we cry out, Daddy Father!

The same Spirit testifies together with our spirit that we are God's offspring.

If we are offspring, also heirs, heirs of God, and co-heirs of the Anointed King if indeed we co-suffer, in order that we would also be co-glorified.

And likewise the Spirit assists in our weaknesses; for we have not perceived what we should necessarily pray about, but the same Spirit super-intercedes on our behalf in unutterable groanings[224]

To the only wise God our liberator be glory and

majesty, might and authority, even now and into all the ages; amen![225]

Sixth Day – 2nd Hour

In my distress I cried out before the LORD, and he heard me.

Deliver my soul, O LORD, from lying lips, and from a deceitful tongue.

O deceitful tongue, what will be given to you? or what shall be added to you?

Sharpened arrows are of the mighty one, with wilderness coals.

Alas, for my sojourn was lengthened, I encamped with the tents of Kedar.

Long was my soul exiled!

I was peaceful with those who hate peace; when I was speaking with them, they were battling me unjustly.[226]

Praise ye the LORD. O give thanks to the LORD, for he is good, for into the coming age is his deliverance.

Who will tell the dominant deeds of the LORD, and make all his praises heard?

Blessed are those who keep justice and do righteousness in every season.

Be mindful of us in goodwill for your people,

O LORD, visit us with your liberation,

To see the kindness of your chosen ones, to rejoice in the rejoicing of your nation, to be celebrated with your inheritance.

With our fathers we sinned, we transgressed, we did injustice.

In Egypt our fathers did not comprehend your marvelous deeds, they were not mindful of the plenitude of your aid, and they provoked you while going up in the red sea.

They did not completely destroy the nations, which the LORD spoke to them,

And they were mingled among the nations and learned their works;

And they slaved unto their carved objects, and it became into a trap for them;

And they sacrificed their sons and their daughters to the demons

And poured out innocent blood, blood of their sons and of their daughters, whom they sacrificed to the carved objects of Canaan; and the land was polluted by the blood

And it was stained by their works, and they practiced whoredom by their pursuits.

Liberate us, O LORD our God, and gather us out of the nations, to give thanks unto your holy name, to leap joyfully in your praise!

Blessed be the Lord God of Israel from age until age. and all the people will say, amen amen![227]

Sixth Day – 3rd Hour

It was the third hour, and they crucified him.

And the inscription of his accusation was having been inscribed: The King of the Jews.[228]

O God, give your judgment to the king and your righteousness to the king's son,

To judge your people in righteousness, and your poor ones in judgment.

Let the mountains take up peace for your people, and let the hills do so in righteousness!

He will judge the poor of the people and liberate the children of the needy and humble the accuser,

And he will endure with the sun and will be before the moon for generations of generations,

And he will descend as rain upon the fleece and as droplets dropping upon the land.

In his days, righteousness will arise and a plenitude of peace, until when the moon would be taken away.

And he will overrule from sea to sea, and from

the river to the rivers of the world.

Ethiopians will fall down before him, and his enemies will lick the dust.

The islands and the kings of Tarshish will offer gifts; the kings of Arabia and Sheba will bring forth gifts;

And all the kings will bow down to him; all the nations will slave unto him.

Because he rushed the poor one out of a ruler's hand, even the needy one for whom there was not a rescuer;

He will spare the poor and needy one, and he will liberate the souls of the needy;

He will ransom their souls out of usury and injustice, and their name will be valuable in his sight.

And he will live, and it shall be given to him from the gold of Arabia, and they will pray about him through everything; they will praise him the whole day.

There will be sustenance in the land upon the peaks of the mountains; its fruit will exceed above Lebanon, and they will bloom forth out of a city like grass from the ground.

His name be blessed into the ages! his name will continue before the sun, and all the tribes of the land will be blessed in him; all the nations will bless him.

Blessed be the LORD God, the God of Israel, the only one who does marvelous things,

And blessed be the name of his glory into the coming age and into age of age, and the whole land shall be filled of his glory. amen, amen![229]

Halleluiah! praise the LORD, all ye nations; applaud him, all ye peoples;

For his lovingkindness was determined toward us, and the truth of the LORD continues into the age to come.[230]

Sixth Day – 4th Hour

I expected upon you, O LORD; into the coming age, let me not be turned away; rescue me and lift me away in your righteousness.

Incline your ear toward me, hasten to take me away! become God my overshielder and a house of refuge to save me.

For you yourself are my might and my refuge, and for your name's sake you will guide me and sustain me;

Lead me out of this trap which they hid for me, because you yourself are my overshielder.

Into your hands I will present my spirit; you ransomed me, O LORD, the God of truth.

I hated those who preoccupy themselves with frivolities through emptiness; yet as for me, I hoped upon the LORD.

I will leap joyfully and make merry at your aid, for you looked upon my humility; you liberated my soul out of compulsions

And did not enclose me in the hands of an enemy; but you stationed my feet in an open space.

Rescue me, LORD, for I am compressed; troubled by sorrow was my eye, my soul and my stomach.

For my life gave out in distress, and my years amid sighing; my strength weakened in poverty, and my bones were troubled.

I became a disgrace in the presence of my enemies and exceedingly so to my neighbors, even a dread to my acquaintances; those who observed me outside fled away from me.

I was forgotten from heart like a dead person; I became like a weapon having been destroyed.

For I heard blame from the many who dwell all around; when they were gathered together against me, they plotted to take my soul.

Yet I expected upon you, O LORD. I said, You are my God.

My seasons are in your hands; rush me out of

the hand of my enemies and from those who pursue me.

Shine your face upon your slave, save me by your lovingkindness.

O LORD, may I not be turned away, for I called upon you; let the irreverent ones be turned away and led down into hades.

O let the deceitful lips become speechless, which speak lawlessness against the righteous in arrogance and scorn.

O LORD, how vast is the plenitude of your kindness which you hid within those who fear you! you produced it in those who expect upon you in front of the children of men.

In the shelter of your face you will hide them from the turmoil of men; you will cover them in a tent away from the tongues of contradiction.

O blessed be the LORD, for he made marvelous his lovingkindness in a city of fortification.

Yet I said in my astonishment, I have been cast off from before your eyes. therefore when I had cried out to you, you listened to the voice of my pleading.

Love the LORD, all his saints, for the LORD seeks out truth, and he repays to those who exert arrogance abundantly.

Be valorous, all who expect upon the LORD, and

may your heart be empowered![231]

Sixth Day – 5th Hour

Halleluia! I loved, because the LORD will listen to the voice of my pleading,

For he inclined his ear toward me, and I in my days will call upon him.

The birth pangs of death surrounded me, and the dangers of hades found me; I found oppression and distress.

And I invoked the name of the LORD, saying, Deliver my soul, O LORD!

The LORD is rescuing and righteous, and our God rescues.

Guarding the childlike ones is the LORD; I was humbled, and he liberated me.

O my soul, return into your rest, for the LORD did well to you,

For he lifted my soul out of death, my eyes from tears, and my feet from slipping.

In the land of the living, I should be well pleasing before the LORD.[232]

Master, if you would desire, you are able to cleanse me.

Master, I will journey with you to wherever you would go.

Master Jesus, rescue us!

Jesus Son of David, rescue me!

Son of David, rescue me![233]

Halleluiah! I trusted, therefore I spoke; yet I was greatly humiliated.

I said in my astonishment, Every person is a liar.

What will I repay to the LORD for all the things which he rendered to me?

I will take the cup of liberation, and I will call upon the name of the LORD.

Precious before the LORD is the death of his holy ones.

O LORD, I am your slave; I am your slave and a child of your maidservant; you broke through my chains,

I will sacrifice a sacrifice of praise to you;

I will render my vows to the LORD in front of all his people

In the courts of the house of the LORD, in your midst, O Jerusalem![234]

Sixth Day – 6th Hour

Of the passover festival, it was being the day of Sabbath preparation, but about the sixth hour; and he says to the Jews, Behold, he is your king.

They screamed, Take up, take up, crucify him! Pilate says to them, Will I crucify your king? the archministers replied, We do not have a king except Caesar.[235]

The LORD said to my Lord, Sit from my right hand, until I would place your enemies as a footstool of your feet.

The LORD will dispatch your rod of power out of Zion. rule in the midst of your enemies!

The beginning is with you in the day of your power, amid the radiances of the holy ones; before the morning star was, I begot you from the womb.

The LORD has sworn and will not regret: You, you are a minister into the coming age according to the order of Melchizedek.

The Lord from your right hand shattered kings in a day of his anger;

He will judge among the nations, he will fill them with corpses; he will crush upon the land the heads of many.

In the path he will drink out of the brook, therefore he will uplift his head.[236]

To you a hymn is proper in Zion, O God, and to you a vow will be rendered in Jerusalem.

Listen closely to my prayer: All flesh will draw near to you.

Words of transgressions overpowered us, and you will pardon our irreverent deeds.

Blessed is the one whom you preferred and brought in; he will encamp in your courts. we will be filled with the good things of your house; holy is your temple, marvelous in righteousness.

Heed us, O God our savior, the hope of all the edges of the land and far off in the sea,

Who prepares mountains in his strength, who was clothed in sovereignty,

Who stirs the vault of the sea, the sounds of its waves. the nations will be stirred,

And those who inhabit the edges of the land will be frightened of your signs; yet you will enjoy the processions of morning and evening.

You visited the land and intoxicated it, you repeated enriching it; the river of God was filled with waters; you readied their nourishment, for your readiness is so.

O intoxicate the furrows of the land, and multiply its produce! while sprouting forth, it will rejoice amid the raindrops.

From your kindness, you will bless the crown of the year, and your plains will be filled of richness;

The ripened goods of the wilderness will be enriched, and the hills will be wrapped with exultation.

The rams of the sheep were clothed, and the valleys multiplied their grain; they will shout, and indeed they will sing hymns![237]

Rabbi, you are the Son of God; you are the King of Israel!

Hosanna! blessed is the King of Israel, the one who comes in the name of the Lord!

Blessed is the King who comes in the name of the Lord; peace in heaven, and glory in the highest!

Be mindful of me, Lord, when you would come in your kingdom![238]

Sixth Day – 7th Hour

From the sixth hour, darkness became over all the land until the ninth hour.[239]

Anointed King Jesus, who was existing in God's form, did not deem it a theft to be equal to God,

But he emptied himself, taking the form of a slave, becoming in the likeness of humans,

And being found in form as a human, he lowered himself, becoming obedient until death, yet the death of a cross.

Therefore God highly elevated him and granted to him the name above every name,

So that in the name of Jesus, every knee would bend, of those in heaven and on earth and under the earth,

And every tongue would agree aloud that Anointed King Jesus is Master for the glory of Father God.[240]

O God, you would not silently pass by my praise,

For the mouth of a sinner and the mouth of a deceiver were opened up against me, they spoke against me in a deceitful tongue

And encircled me in words of hatred and battled me without cause.

In return for love, they were slandering me, yet I was praying;

And they set against me evil things in return for good, and hatred in return for my love.

And you, O Lord GOD, show compassion with me for the sake of your name, because your compassion is good!

Deliver me, for I myself am poor and needy,

and my heart has been agitated within me.

I was taken away like a shadow in its reclining; I was shaken off like a locust.

My knees were weakened from fasting, and my flesh was altered in regard to its shine.

And I myself became a reproach to them; they saw me, they shook their heads.

Rescue me, O LORD my God! liberate me according to your aid,

And let them know that this is your hand, and that you, O LORD, did it.

They will curse, yet you will bless; let those who rise up against me be turned away ashamed, but let your slave rejoice!

Let those who slander me be clothed with embarrassment, and let them wrap themselves in their shame as if a double cloak.

Vehemently will I sing praise to the LORD in my mouth and praise him in the midst of the many,

For he stood by at the right hand of the needy one, to liberate me from those who pursue my soul.[241]

Sixth Day – 8th Hour

Blessed be the God and Father of our Master Anointed King Jesus, the one regenerating us according to his powerful rescue into a living expectation through the resurrection of Anointed King Jesus from the dead;

As many as were baptized into Anointed King Jesus, we were baptized into his death

In the Name of the Father and of the Son and the Holy Spirit

The Encourager,

The Comforter,

The Exhorter, the Spirit of truth who proceeds from the Father

And he will convict the world about sin and righteousness and judgment.

The Lord is the Spirit; yet where the Spirit of the Lord is, freedom is there.

For these are God's children, as many as are led by God's Spirit

The Spirit of adoption, in whom we cry out, Daddy Father!

The same Spirit testifies together with our spirit that we are God's offspring.

If we are offspring, also heirs, heirs of God, and co-heirs of the Anointed King if indeed we co-suffer, in order that we would also be co-glorified.

And likewise the Spirit assists in our weaknesses; for we have not perceived what we should necessarily pray about, but the same Spirit super-intercedes on our behalf in unutterable groanings[242]

If it were not that the LORD was among us, indeed let Israel say;

If it were not that the LORD was among us while men were rising up against us,

Then they would have consumed us alive while their anger was raging against us;

Then the waters would have drowned us, our soul would have passed through a surge;

Then our soul would have passed through the overwhelming water.

Blessed be the LORD, who did not give us as a victim for their teeth.

Our soul was delivered like a sparrow out of the trap of those who hunt it; the trap was crushed, and we were delivered.

Our rescue is in the name of the LORD, who made heaven and earth.[243]

Holy, holy, holy is the Lord God the Omnipotence, who was and is and is coming.

Let there be glory and honor and gratitude to the one sitting upon the throne, he who lives into the ages of ages,

Worthy are you the Holy One, our Master and God, to take the glory and the honor and the the power; for you created all things, and they existed and were created because of your will![244]

Sixth Day – 9th Hour

About the ninth hour, Jesus shouted in a great voice, saying, Eli Eli lima sabachthani? This is, My God my God, why did you abandon me?[245]

Not to us, O LORD, not to us but to your name, give glory to your compassion and your truth,

Lest the nations should say, Where is their God?

Yet our God is in heaven above; he made all things in the heavens and in the earth, as many things as he willed.

The idols of the nations are silver and gold, the works of the hands of people;

They have mouths and will not speak, they have eyes and will not see,

They have ears and will not hear, they have noses and will not smell,

They have hands and they will not touch, they have feet and will not walk, they will not make a noise in their throat.

O that those who make them would become like them, and all those who trust upon them.

The house of Israel hoped upon the LORD; he is their rescuer and their overshielder.

The house of Aaron hoped upon the LORD; he is their rescuer and their overshielder.

Those who fear the LORD hoped upon the LORD; he is their rescuer and their overshielder.

The LORD was mindful of us and blessed us, he blessed the house of Israel, he blessed the house of Aaron,

He blessed those who fear the LORD, the small ones with the great ones.

May the LORD give more to you, to you and to your children;

You are blessed by the LORD who made heaven and earth.

The sky of the heaven is the LORD's; yet he gave the land to the children of men.

The dead will not praise you, O LORD, nor all those who descend into hades,

But we who live shall bless the LORD from now until the coming age![246]

Worthy are you to take the scroll and to open up its seals, for you were butchered, and with your blood you purchased us unto God out of every tribe and tongue and people and nation,

And you made them kings and ministers to our God; and they will reign upon the earth.

Worthy is the little Lamb, the one having been butchered, to get the power and the fullness and wisdom and strength and honor and glory and blessing.

To the One sitting upon the throne and to the little Lamb be the blessing and the honor and the glory and the might into the ages of ages![247]

Sixth Day – Intercession Hour

Concerning you, I have pleaded that your trust would not fail; and you, when you turn back, strengthen your siblings![248]

Our Master Anointed King Jesus and our God and Father who loves us with generosity and who gives us timeless encouragement and good hope,

May he encourage your hearts and stabilize you in every good word and work.[249]

Blessed are the poor, for the kingdom of God is yours.

Blessed are those who hunger now, for you will be satisfied. blessed are those who sob now, for you will laugh.

Blessed are you whenever people would hate you and exclude you and insult you and reject your name as evil because of the son of man.

Rejoice and leap joyfully in that day, for your payment in heaven is much, for their fathers were doing the same things to the prophets.[250]

I lifted my eyes into the hills. from where does my rescue arrive?

My rescue is from the LORD who made the heaven and the earth.

He would not give your foot into shaking, nor would he lull the one who guards you.

Behold, he who guards Israel will neither tire nor slumber.

The LORD guards you, the LORD is your shelter at your right hand.

The sun will not enflame you by day, nor will the moon enflame the night.

The LORD will guard you from every evil; he shall guard your soul.

The LORD will guard your entryway and your exit-way from now and until the age to come.[251]

May our God and Father himself and our

Master Anointed King Jesus straighten out our path toward you;

And may the Master make you overflowing and exceeding of what is necessary, in love for one another and for all people, just as indeed we also do for you,

In order to stabilize your hearts as blameless in holiness before our God and Father amid the coming of our Master Anointed King Jesus with all his saints.[252]

May the God of peace hallow you completely, and may your whole spirit and soul and body be guarded blamelessly in the presence of our Master Anointed King Jesus.

Trustworthy is the one who calls you, who will also do it.

The generosity of our Master Anointed King Jesus be with you; amen.[253]

Sixth Day – 11th Hour

O sing praise to the LORD, for he is good, for into the coming age is his deliverance!

Indeed let those who fear the LORD say that he is good, for into the coming age is his deliverance!

In narrow straights I called upon the LORD, and into an open space he heard from me.

The LORD is my rescuer, I shall not fear; what will a human do to me?

The LORD is my rescuer, and I myself will oversee my enemies.

It is better to have trusted upon the LORD than to have trusted upon man;

It is better to have trusted upon the LORD than to have placed hope upon rulers;

Being forced back, I was tripped up to fall, and the LORD took hold of me.

My strength and my song is the LORD, and he became my liberation.

In the tents of the righteous is a voice of rejoicing and liberation: The right hand of the LORD composed power,

The right hand of the LORD uplifted me, the right hand of the LORD composed power.

I will not die, but I will live and recount the works of the LORD.

Chastening, the LORD chastened me and did not deliver me over to death.

Open up to me the gates of righteousness! entering in them, I will sing praise unto the LORD.

This is the gate of the LORD; righteous ones will enter by it.

I will sing praise to you, for you heard from me

and became my liberation.

A stone which the builders rejected, this became the head cornerstone;

This happened from the LORD, and it is marvelous in our eyes.

This is the day which the LORD made; we should leap joyfully and be gladdened by it.

O LORD, liberate indeed; O LORD, prosper indeed!

He has been blessed who comes in the name of the LORD; we have blessed you from the house of the LORD.

God is the LORD, and he appeared for us; put together a feast among the covered places as far as the horns of the altar.

You are my God, and I will sing praise to you; you are my God, I will exalt you; I will sing praise to you, because you heard from me and became my liberation.

O sing praise to the LORD, for he is good, for into the coming age is his deliverance![254]

Sixth Day – 12th Hour

Rebuke me not, O LORD, in your passion, nor chasten me in your anger.

Rescue me, O LORD, for I am feeble; heal me, O LORD, for my bones are disturbed,

And my soul is vehemently disturbed; and as for you, O LORD, how long?

Turn back, O LORD, deliver my soul, liberate me because of your compassion!

For in death there is not one who is mindful of you; yet who will give thanks to you in hades?

I toiled in my groaning; every night I will bathe my bed, in tears I will drench my pallet.

My eye was troubled from passion; I was made old by all my enemies.

Depart from me, all ye who work lawlessness! for the LORD listened to the sound of my sobbing;

The LORD hearkened to my pleading, the LORD received my prayer.

O that all my enemies would be ashamed and vehemently troubled; may they be turned away, and with swiftness may they be vehemently put to shame.[255]

Behold indeed, bless the LORD, all ye slaves of the LORD who have stood in the house of the LORD in the courts of our God.

In the night times, lift up your hands in the sanctuary and bless the LORD!

Out of Zion, the LORD who made heaven and earth will bless you.[256]

Out of the deep I cried aloud to you, O LORD.

Master, listen to my voice; let your ears become attentive unto the voice of my pleading.

LORD, if you should watch closely for transgression, O Lord, who will stand up?

Because the pleaser, he is beside you.

I awaited you on account of your law, O LORD; my soul waited for your word.

From the watch of early morning until the night, my soul expected upon the Lord; from the watch of early morning, let Israel expect upon the LORD!

Because the deliverance, he is beside the LORD, even a plenteous ransom, he is beside him,

And he himself will ransom Israel out of all his transgressions.[257]

Seventh Day – 1ˢᵗ Hour

Awake O sleeper and arise from the dead, and the Anointed King will shine upon you.[258]

Blessed be the God and Father of our Master Anointed King Jesus, the one regenerating us according to his powerful rescue into a living expectation through the resurrection of Anointed King Jesus from the dead;

As many as were baptized into Anointed King Jesus, we were baptized into his death

In the Name of the Father and of the Son and the Holy Spirit

The Encourager,

The Comforter,

The Exhorter, the Spirit of truth who proceeds from the Father

And he will convict the world about sin and righteousness and judgment.

The Lord is the Spirit; yet where the Spirit of the Lord is, freedom is there.

For these are God's children, as many as are led by God's Spirit

The Spirit of adoption, in whom we cry out, Daddy Father!

The same Spirit testifies together with our spirit that we are God's offspring.

If we are offspring, also heirs, heirs of God, and co-heirs of the Anointed King if indeed we co-suffer, in order that we would also be co-glorified.

And likewise the Spirit assists in our weaknesses; for we have not perceived what we should necessarily pray about, but the same Spirit super-intercedes on our behalf in unutterable groanings[259]

Lord, my heart was not lofty, nor were my eyes elevated, neither did I proceed in great matters, nor things marvelous above me.

If I was not being humble minded, but elevated my soul like a weaned child against his mother, then it is like a retribution against my own soul.

Let Israel expect upon the LORD from the present until the coming age.[260]

Even until the present hour we hunger and thirst and go naked and roam and are beaten;

And we tire, working with our own hands; being insulted, we bless; being persecuted, we endure, being despised, we encourage;

We were made to become like the abhorrences of the world, the scum of all things until the present time.[261]

To the one who loves us and washes us from our sins in his blood, Anointed King Jesus, the trustworthy witness, the first born from the dead, and the Ruler of the kings of the earth.

Into ages of ages, let the glory and the power be unto him who made us a kingdom, as ministers unto his God and Father; amen.[262]

Seventh Day – 2nd Hour

Halleluiah! O servants, praise the LORD, praise the name of the LORD;

O may the name of the LORD have been blessed from the present and until the coming age;

From the sun's risings as far as its settings, praise the name of the LORD!

The LORD is lofty toward all the nations, and his glory toward the heavens.

Who is like the LORD our God who dwells in the heights

And oversees the lowly things in the sky and in the land?

He is the one who rouses the poor person from the land and elevates the needy one from the dunghill

To seat him with the rulers, with the rulers of his people;

He is the one who settles the barren woman in a home like a rejoicing mother of children.[263]

Our Father in heaven, your name be hallowed,
Your kingdom come, and your will happen on earth as it does in heaven,
Give us today our daily bread,
And release for us our debts, as we ourselves also release our debtors;
And bring us not into testing, but rush us away from the evil one. for yours is the kingdom and the power and the glory into the ages; amen![264]

Because you heard the words of my mouth, I will sing praise to you with my whole heart, and I will strum to you in front of the angels.
I will bow down toward your holy temple and sing praise to your name for your compassion and your truth, because you magnified your revelation over every name.
In whatever day I would call upon you, heed me swiftly! with power you will prosper me in my soul.
Let all the kings of the land sing praise to you, O Lᴏʀᴅ, because they heard all the utterances of your mouth,
And let them sing in the paths of the Lᴏʀᴅ, for

great is the glory of the Lord,

For the Lord is lofty and watches over the lowly things, and he knows the lofty things from afar.

If I should proceed in the midst of affliction, you will enliven me; you stretched out your hand against the wrath of my enemies, and your right hand liberated me!

The Lord will repay on my behalf. O Lord, into the coming age is your lovingkindness; you would not neglect the works of your hands.[265]

Seventh Day – 3rd Hour

Remove me, O Lord, from an evil person, rush me away from an unjust man,

Those who calculated injustice in their heart were arranging battles the whole day;

They sharpened their tongues like that of a serpent, the poison of cobras was under their lips.

O Lord, guard me from the hands of a sinner, remove me from an unjust person, from those who plotted to trip my footsteps;

The arrogant hid a trap for me and extended ropes as traps for my feet, they set things upon the path as a stumbling block for me.

I spoke to the Lord: You are my God! give ear, O Lord, to the sound of my pleading.

O Lord GOD, the power of my liberation, you overshadowed my head in the day of war.

Deliver me not from my desire, O LORD, to a sinner; they disputed against me; you would not abandon me, lest they be exalted.

I knew that the LORD will render the judgment of an impoverished man and the justice of the needy ones.

Surely the righteous ones will give thanks to your name, and the upright will dwell together in your presence.[266]

Praise ye the LORD, because a psalm is good; and may this praise be made sweet unto our God.

The LORD constructs Jerusalem and will gather together the dispersions of Israel,

He who heals the crushed in the heart and who binds up their fractures,

Who counts the multitudes of the stars, and he designates names for them all.

Great is our Lord, and great is his strength; and none can quantify his comprehension.

He is the LORD, uplifting the meek, but lowering sinners to the ground.

Start out with thanksgiving unto the LORD; with a harp, strum ye unto our God,

To him who wraps the sky with clouds, to the one who prepares rain for the land, to the one who sprouts forth grass upon the mountains and green herbs for the service of people,

To him who gives the animals their nourishment, even the hatchlings of ravens which call upon him.

He delights not in the power of the horse, nor takes pleasure in the legs of a man;

The LORD takes pleasure in those who fear him, those who expect upon his lovingkindness.[267]

Seventh Day – 4th Hour

Unto you, O LORD, I lift my soul, O my God.

I trust upon you; O may I not be turned back ashamed, nor let my enemies make a mockery of me.

Yet indeed, all those who await you could not be turned back ashamed; let those who rebel in futility be turned back ashamed.

Make known to me your paths, O LORD, and teach me your trails!

Guide me upon your truth and teach me, for you yourself are God my liberator, and I await you the whole day.

Be mindful, O LORD, of your pities and your lovingkindnesses, for they are from of old.

Be not mindful of the sins and ignorance of my youth; be mindful of me according to your lovingkindess because of your goodness, O LORD.

Good and upright is the LORD; therefore he will frame laws for those who sin in the path.

He will guide the meek in their decision, he will teach the meek his paths.

All the paths of the LORD are lovingkindness and truth for those who keep his covenant and his testimonies.

For your name's sake, you will be merciful to my sin, O LORD; because my sin is great.

Who is a person who fears the LORD? he will frame laws for him in the path which he chose.

His soul will encamp among good things, and his seed will inherit the land.

The power of the LORD belongs to those who fear him, and the name of the LORD to those who fear him; and his covenant exists to clarify for them.

My eyes are toward the LORD through everything, for he will pull my feet out from a trap.

O look upon me and rescue me, for I myself am an only child and poor.

The afflictions of my heart were broadened; O

lead me out from my compulsions.

Behold my humiliation and my pain, and release all my sins!

Behold my enemies, for they were multiplied and hated me with a cruel hatred.

Guard my soul and deliver me; let me not be turned back ashamed, for I expected upon you.

Innocent and upright people were cleaving to me, because I awaited you, O Lord.

O God, ransom Israel out of all his afflictions.[268]

Seventh Day – 5th Hour

In my voice I cried out to the LORD; in my voice I pleaded before the LORD.

I will pour out my pleading before him; in his presence I will report my afflictions.

While my spirit was fainting away from me, you also knew my tracks; they hid a trap for me in this path in which I was going.

Toward my right hand I was discerning and observing that there was no one who recognizes me; a refuge was lost from me, and there was no one who looks out for my soul.

I cried out to you, O LORD; I said, You are my expectation, my portion in the land of the living!

Attend to my pleading, for I was severely

humiliated; rush me out from those who persecute me, for they were empowered over me.

Lord, bring forth my soul out of prison, to sing praise unto your name; the righteous will wait for me until you respond to me.[269]

To the only wise God our liberator be glory and majesty, might and authority, even now and into all the ages; amen![270]

Halleluiah! praise ye the LORD from the heavens, praise him in the heights.

Praise him, all his angels; praise him, all his armies.

Praise him, sun and moon; praise him, all the stars of light.

Praise him, O heavens of the heavens, and O water above the skies.

Let them praise the name of the LORD, for he spoke and they became; he commanded, and they were created.

He established these things into the coming age and into age of age; he placed a decree, and it shall not pass away.

Praise the LORD from the earth, ye dragons and all the deeps,

Fire, hail, snow, ice, hurricane wind, the things
which do his word,

The mountains and all the hills, fruitful trees
and all cedars,

Wild beasts and all the animals, creeping things
and winged birds,

Kings of the land and all peoples, rulers and all
the judges of the land,

Young men and virgins, elders with the youths;

Let them praise the name of the LORD, for his
name alone was exalted; the acknowledgement
of him is upon the land and the sky.

And he will exalt the horn of his people; a
hymn is within all his saints, the children of
Israel, a people which draws near unto him.[271]

Seventh Day – 6th Hour

Rabbi, you are the Son of God; you are the
King of Israel!

Truly you are God's Son.

You are the Anointed King, the Son of the
living God.

Yes Lord, I have trusted that you are the
Anointed King, the Son of God, the one coming
into the world.

Master, I will journey with you to wherever you
would go.

We are unworthy slaves, for we have only done those things which we were required to do.

Master, to whom will we go? you have the utterances of timeless life;

And we have trusted and known that you are the Anointed King the Son of the living God.[272]

Blessed be the LORD my God, who teaches my hands for the battleline, and my fingers for war;

O LORD, what is a human, that you knew him, or the son of a human, that you make account of him?

Humanity was made as futility, his days go by as if a shadow.

O LORD, bend down your heavens and descend; touch the mountains, and they will smoke!

Flash your lightning, and you will scatter them; dispatch your arrows, and you will confuse them!

Dispatch your hand out of the heights; take me and rush me out from many waters, from the hand of the children of strangers

Whose mouth spoke futility, and whose right hand was the right hand of injustice.

O God, I will sing a new song to you, I will strum with a ten-stringed instrument to you,

The one who gives liberation to the kings, who

ransoms his servant David from a wicked sword.

Rush me away and lift me out of the hand of the children of strangers, whose mouth spoke futility, and whose right hand was the right hand of injustice.

Their sons are like new sprouts having ripened in their youth, their daughters having been beautified and adorned like the image of a palace,

Their treasuries are full and spewing forth from here to there, their sheep are plentiful and multiplying in their streets,

Their oxen are thick, there is no collapse of a fence nor highway, nor is there an outcry in their streets,

They count blessed the people for whom these things are so; yet blessed is the people whose God is the LORD.[273]

Seventh Day – 7th Hour

I will exalt you, O my God my king; and I will bless your name into age of age.

Every day will I bless you, and I will praise your name into the coming age and into age of age.

Great is the LORD and greatly praiseworthy, and there is no end of his majesty.

Generation and generation will praise your works and declare your power.

They will speak the magnificence of the glory of your holiness, and they will recount your marvelous deeds.

They will speak the power of your formidable deeds and recount your majesty.

They will erupt with the memory of the plenitude of your kindness and will leap joyfully in your righteousness.

The LORD is pitying and compassionate, long suffering and greatly compassionate.

The LORD is altogether kind in all things, and his compassions are upon all of his works.

O LORD, let all your works sing praise to you, and your saints bless you!

They will utter the glory of your kingdom and speak of your dominant deeds,

So that your dominant deeds and the glory of the majesty of your kingdom would be made known to the children of men.

Your kingdom is a kingdom of all the ages, and your dominion is among every generation and generation.

The LORD is trustworthy in his words, and holy in all his works.

The LORD undergirds all those who fall down,

and he sets upright all those having been broken down.

The eyes of all things hope for you, and you give their nourishment in due season.

Out of goodwill, you open up your hand and fill every living thing.

Righteous in all his paths is the LORD, and holy in all of his works.

Near is the LORD to all those who call upon him, to all those who call upon him in truth.

He will do the desire of those who fear him, and he will listen to their pleading and save them.

The LORD guards all those who love him, and he will destroy all the sinful ones.

My mouth will tell the praise of the LORD; let all flesh bless his holy name into age of age.[274]

Seventh Day – 8th Hour

My soul magnifies the Lord

And my spirit has rejoiced in God my liberator,

For he looked upon the lowliness of his slave.

For the powerful one did great things for me, and holy is his name.

And his mercy is for generations of generations to those who fear him.

He performed mighty deeds by his arm, he scattered haughty ones in the thinking of their hearts.

He took down rulers from thrones and elevated the lowly ones.

He filled hungering ones of good things, and those who were being enriched he sent out empty.[275]

Halleluiah! praise the LORD, O Jerusalem; praise your God, O Zion,

For he strengthened the bars of your gates; he blessed your children within you;

The one who appoints peace for your borders and fills you with the fat of wheat;

Who sends forth his oracle upon the land, for the swift running of his word.

He is the one who announces his word to Jacob, his statutes and judgments to Israel.

He did not work in this manner with every nation, and he did not clarify his judgments to them.[276]

Blessed are the poor in spirit, for theirs is the kingdom of the heavens.

Blessed are those who grieve, for they shall be encouraged.

Blessed are the meek, for they will inherit the land.

Blessed are those who hunger and thirst for righteousness, for they will be satisfied.

Blessed are those who rescue, for they will be rescued.

Blessed are the clean in heart, for they will see God.

Blessed are those who make peace, for they shall be called God's children.

Blessed those having been persecuted because of righteousness, for theirs is the kingdom of the heavens.[277]

Seventh Day – 9th Hour

Blessed be the God and Father of our Master Anointed King Jesus, the one regenerating us according to his powerful rescue into a living expectation through the resurrection of Anointed King Jesus from the dead;

As many as were baptized into Anointed King Jesus, we were baptized into his death

In the Name of the Father and of the Son and the Holy Spirit

The Encourager,

The Comforter,

The Exhorter, the Spirit of truth who proceeds

from the Father

And he will convict the world about sin and righteousness and judgment.

The Lord is the Spirit; yet where the Spirit of the Lord is, freedom is there.

For these are God's children, as many as are led by God's Spirit

The Spirit of adoption, in whom we cry out, Daddy Father!

The same Spirit testifies together with our spirit that we are God's offspring.

If we are offspring, also heirs, heirs of God, and co-heirs of the Anointed King if indeed we co-suffer, in order that we would also be co-glorified.

And likewise the Spirit assists in our weaknesses; for we have not perceived what we should necessarily pray about, but the same Spirit super-intercedes on our behalf in unutterable groanings[278]

Halleluiah! praise the LORD, O my soul.

I will I praise the LORD in my life, I will strum to my God as long as I exist.

Do not hold confidence upon rulers and upon the sons of men, in whom there is no deliverance.

His breath will go out, and he will return into his ground; in that day their debates will perish.

Happy is he whose rescuer is the God of Jacob, whose expectation is upon the LORD his God,

The one who made the sky and the land and the sea and all the things in them, the one who guards truth into the coming age,

Who makes a judgment for those who are being harmed, who gives nourishment to those who hunger; the LORD releases those who have been shackled,

The LORD sets upright those who were broken down, the LORD makes wise the blind, the LORD loves the righteous;

The LORD guards the immigrants; he will uplift the orphan and widow, and he will obscure the path of sinners.

The LORD your God will reign into the coming age, O Zion, for generation and generation.[279]

Seventh Day – Intercession Hour

May the God of peace, who brought up from the dead our Master Jesus the great shepherd of the sheep by the blood of the timeless covenant,

May he equip you in every good work to do his desire, doing in you what is well-pleasing in his presence through Anointed King Jesus, to whom be the glory into ages of ages; amen![280]

May the LORD hear you in the day of affliction; may the name of the God of Jacob shield you.

May he dispatch aid to you from the sanctuary; and out of Zion, may he assist you.

May he be mindful of your every sacrifice and cherish your whole burnt offering.

May he give to you according to your heart and fulfill your every intention.

We will rejoice in your rescue, and we will boast in the name of our God; may the LORD fulfill all your requests.

Now I knew that the LORD saved his anointed one; he will heed him from his holy heaven; in his sovereignty is the liberation of his right hand.

They boast in chariots, and others in horses; yet we will boast the name of the LORD our God.

They were footbound and fell, yet we rose again and were set upright.

O LORD, save your king and heed us in the day we call upon you.[281]

From the day we heard, we do not stop praying on your behalf and asking that you would be filled with the recognition of his will in all wisdom and spiritual comprehension,

For you to walk worthily of the Master, for all desire to please, bringing forth fruit in every good work and growing into the recognition of God,

Being empowered in all power according to the might of his glory into all endurance and long-suffering with gladness,

Thanking the Father who enables us for the sharing of the inheritance of the saints in light,

Who rushed us out of the authority of darkness and transferred us into the kingdom of his beloved Son,

In whom we have the ransom payment, the release of sins;

Who is the icon of the invisible God, the firstborn of all creation,

Because all things visible and invisible were created by him in heaven and on earth, whether thrones or lordships, whether rulers or authorities, all things were created through him and for him,

And he is before all things, and all things have taken shape in him,

And he is the head of the body, the congregation; he who is the beginning, the firstborn out of the dead, in order that he would become foremost in all things

Because all the fullness was pleased to dwell in him

And through him to fully change all things for him, making peace through the blood of his cross; all things through him, whether things on earth or in the heavens.[282]

Seventh Day – 11th Hour

Great and marvelous are your works, Lord God Omnipotence. righteous and true are your paths, O King of the nations.

Lord, who could not fear and glorify your name? for you alone are pure, for all the nations will arrive and bow down before you, for your decrees were made visible.[283]

O Lord, you tested me and knew me;

You knew my sitting down and my rising, you understood my contemplations from afar;

You tracked out my trail and my staff, and you foresaw all my paths.

For there is not a word in my tongue,

Behold, O LORD, you knew all things, the ends and the beginnings; you formed me and placed your hand upon me.

Your knowledge was made marvelous away from me; it was made mighty, I am not capable toward it.

Where would I go away from your spirit, and where would I flee from your face?

If I should ascend into the heaven, you yourself are there; if I should descend into hades, you are present;

If I should take up my wings at dawn and encamp in the ends of the sea,

Even there your hand will indeed guide me, and your right hand will restrain me.

And I said, Surely darkness will trample me down, and amid my delight the night will be light;

For darkness will not be darkened from you, and night will be illuminated like day; as its darkness is, so also is its light.

For you possessed my inmost parts, you assisted me from my mother's womb.

I will sing praise to you, for I was fearfully made wondrous; wondrous are your works, and my soul knows very well.

My bone was not concealed from you, which you made in concealment, and my substance in the lowest parts of the earth;

Your eyes saw my undeveloped form, and all

the people will be written upon your scroll; by day they will be formed, and no one will be formed by them.

Yet to me your loved ones were greatly valued, O God, their beginnings were greatly strengthened;

I will count them, and they will be multiplied above the sand; I was awakened, and I am still with you.

Test me and know my heart, O God, examine me and know my pathways

And see if a lawless path is in me, and guide me in the timeless path![284]

Seventh Day – 12th Hour

I lift my eyes toward you, the one who dwells in heaven.

Behold, as the eyes of slaves look into their masters' hands, like a maidservant's eyes into her mistress's hands; in this way are our eyes toward the LORD our God until he pities us.

Rescue us, O LORD, rescue us, for we were exceedingly filled of disdain!

Our soul was filled too much. the reproach came from those who prosper, and the disdain from the arrogant.[285]

Listen to my prayer, O Lord; in your faithfulness give ear to my pleading, heed me in your righteousness;

And do not enter into judgment with your slave, for no living person will be counted righteous before you.

For the enemy of my soul sought after me, he debased my life down into the ground; he sat me in shadows like the dead ones of old;

And my spirit grew weary upon me; my heart was disturbed within me.

I was reminded of olden days, and I meditated in all your works; I was meditating in the deeds of your hands.

Toward you, I spread out my hands; my soul was toward you, like earth without water.

Hear me swiftly, O Lord, my spirit fainted; turn not your face away from me, for I would be like those who descend into a pit.

At dawn make your lovingkindness heard to me, for I expected upon you; make known to me the path in which I shall proceed, O Lord, for I lifted my soul toward you;

Lift me away from my enemies, O Lord, for I fled toward you.

Teach me to do your desire; for you are my God; your good spirit will guide me into the land of uprightness.

Enliven me for your name's sake, O LORD, bring my soul out of affliction by your righteousness;

And in your lovingkindness, you will cut off my enemies and destroy all those who afflict my soul; for I am your slave.[286]

Halleluiah! sing a new song unto the LORD; let his praise be amidst the congregation of saints.

Let Israel rejoice before the one who made him, let the children of Zion leap joyfully before their King;

Let them praise his name in dance; with the drum and lyre, let them strum for him.

For the LORD takes pleasure in his people, and he will elevate the meek in liberation.

The holy ones will boast in glory, and they will rejoice upon their beds![287]

Communion Readings

True Meat and True Drink:

I am the living bread descending out of the heaven; if anyone would eat from this bread, he will live into the coming age. the bread which I will give is my flesh, which I will give on behalf of the life of the world.

Firmly firmly I say to you, if you would never eat the flesh of the son of man and drink his blood, you do not have life in yourselves.

The one chewing my flesh and drinking my blood has timeless life, and I will resurrect him in the last day.

For my flesh truly is meat, and my blood truly is drink.

The one chewing my flesh and drinking my blood remains in me, and I in him.

Even as the living Father apostled me, and I live because of the Father, so also will the one who chews on me live because of me.

This is the bread descending out of heaven, not as your fathers ate the manna and died, for the one who chews this bread will live into the coming age.

The spirit is what makes alive, the flesh profits nothing; the statements I speak to you are spirit and life.[288]

<u>Discern the Body of the Master:</u>

Do you not have houses for eating and drinking? or do you despise the congregation of God and shame those who have nothing? What will I say to you? will I commend you in this? I will not commend it.

For I received from the Master what I also deliver to you, that during the night in which he was being betrayed, the Master Jesus took bread and giving thanks he broke it and said,

Take, eat! this is my body being broken on your behalf; do this in my remembrance.

After they were dining, he also took the cup in this way, saying, This cup is the new covenant in my blood; as often as you would ever drink, do this in my remembrance.

For as often as you would eat this bread and drink this cup, you proclaim the Master's death, until whenever he would come.

So also, whoever would eat this bread or drink the cup of the Master unworthily, he will be liable of the Master's body and blood.

A person must test himself, and he must eat out of the bread and drink out of the cup this way.

For the one eating and drinking unworthily eats and drinks judgment to himself, not discerning the Master's body.[289]

<u>Jeremiah & Ezekiel:</u>

Behold, the days are coming, says
the LORD, and I will make a covenant with the
house of Israel and a new covenant with the
house of Judah,

Not according to the covenant which I
covenanted with their fathers in the day I took
their hand to lead them out of the land of
Egypt, for they did not abide in my covenant,
and I did not care for them, says the LORD;

For this is the covenant which I will covenant
with the house of Israel after those days, says
the LORD: Giving, I will give my laws into their
understanding, and I will write them upon their
hearts; and I will be a god for them, and they
will be a people for me

I will give to you a new heart, and I will give
within you a new spirit; I will take the stony
heart out of your flesh and give you a fleshy
heart.

And I will give my Spirit within you, and I will
make it so that you would proceed in my
statutes and closely guard my judgments and
do them.[290]

Covenant with the Vine's New Product:

While they were eating, Jesus, taking the bread and giving thanks, broke it and was giving it to the disciples and said, Take, eat; this is my body.

And taking the cup and giving thanks, he gave to them, saying, All of you, drink from it.

For this is my blood, the blood of the new covenant, being poured out on behalf of many for the release of sins.

I say to you that I could not possibly drink from the product of the vine from now until that day when I drink it newly-made with you in my Father's kingdom.

Singing they came out into the mountain of olives. then Jesus said to them:

In this night, you will all be trapped to stumble away because of me; for it has been written, I will pummel the shepherd, and the sheep of the flock will be scattered;

Yet after I am awakened, I will go before you into Galilee.[291]

Doses of Bread from the Bread of Life:

Behold, that same day two of them were proceeding into a village named Emmaus, seven miles from Jerusalem.

While they were talking and deliberating, it happened that Jesus approached and was proceeding with them.

Yet their eyes were being restrained from recognizing him.

He said to them, What are these words which you exhange with one another as you walk and look sullen?

They said to him, Jesus the Nazarene became a prophet, a man powerful in action and speech before God and all the people,

So that our archpriests and rulers delivered him into a death sentence and crucified him.

He said to them, O mindless ones and slow of heart to trust everything the prophets said!

Wasn't it necessary for the Anointed King to suffer these things and enter into his glory?

Starting from Moses and all the prophets, he was interpreting for them things about himself in all the writings.

It happened while he was reclined with them that he, taking the bread, gave a blessing; and breaking it, he was giving doses to them.

Their eyes were completely opened, and they recognized him; and suddenly he disappeared from them.[292]

<u>Baptism & Bread & Broken Belongings:</u>

And he testified with many other words, and he implored them, saying, Be liberated away from this crooked generation!

Therefore indeed those who were receiving his word in delight were baptized, and about 3,000 souls were adjoined to them in that day.

They were continually persevering in the teaching of the apostles and in the fellowship and in the breaking of bread and in prayers.

Fear became upon every soul, and many miracles and signs were happening through the apostles.

All those who trusted were being together and were holding everything common,

And they were selling their purchases and their belongings, and they were distributing them to everyone according to what anyone needed;

And persevering daily in the temple with one mind, and breaking bread from house to house, they were partaking of food together in rejoicing and in singlemindedness of heart,

Praising God and having generosity toward the whole people. the Master was adding to the congregation daily the ones who were liberated.[293]

<u>Immersed to Crave Spiritual Food & Drink:</u>

Our fathers were being under the cloud, and all came through the sea,

And all were baptized into Moses in the cloud and in the sea,

And all ate the same spiritual food,

And all drank the same spiritual drink; for they were drinking out of an accompanying spiritual rock, yet the rock was being the Anointed King.

But God was not pleased by the majority of them; for they were strewn-down in the wilderness.

These people became our examples, for us not to be cravers of evil things just as those people also craved.

The cup of the blessing—the cup which we bless—is it not a sharing of the blood of the Anointed King? the bread which we break, is it not a sharing of the body of the Anointed King?

Since the bread is one, we the many are one body; for we the many all partake of the one bread.[294]

<u>Drinking the Cup of Enthronement:</u>

Going up to Jerusalem, Jesus took aside the twelve disciples privately in the road and said to them:

Behold, we go up into Jerusalem, and the son of man will be handed over to the archpriests and scribes, and they will condemn him to death;

And they will hand him over to the foreigners to be mocked and flogged and crucified, and he will stand up in the third day.

Then the mother of the sons of Zebedee came before him with her sons, bowing down and asking him for something.

He said to her, What do you desire? She says to him, Say that in your kingdom these my two sons should sit, one from your right and one from your left.

Answering, Jesus said, You know not what you ask. are you able to drink the cup which I myself am about to drink, or to be baptized the baptism which I am baptized? they say to him, We are able.

And he says to them, You will drink my cup, and you will be baptized the baptism which I myself am baptized; yet to sit from my right and from my left is not mine to give, but it is for whom it has been prepared by my Father.

They placed over his head his charge which had been written: This is Jesus the King of the Jews.

Then they crucified with him two thieves, one from his right and one from his left.[295]

Covenant of Free Wine and Food

Ye who thirst, go toward the water! as many of you as walk without money, buy and drink of wine and of fat without money and without price!

Why do you assess value from silver, and your toil does not end in satisfaction? hear from me and eat good things, and your soul will revel in good things!

Hold forth your ears and follow upon my paths; hear from me, and your soul will live amid good things; and I will covenant with you a timeless covenant, the holy and faithful things of David.[296]

End Notes

---

1 Irenaeus, "Against Heresies" book 3, chapter 21, paragraph 4

2 Romans 6:3b-8, 11, 13b

3 Romans 8:29

4 Romans 13:14b

5 Ephesians 4:21-24

6 Ephesians 6:11-18

7 II Corinthians 5:17

8 Colossians 3:1-10

9 II Corinthians 3:18

10 Mark 13:35

11 Matthew 6:9-13

12 LXX Psalm 9:2-15,20-39, corresponds to Masoretic Psalm 9:1-14,19-20; 10:1-18

13 LXX Psalm 21:2-32; corresponds to Masoretic Psalm 22

14 LXX Psalm 101:2-23, 26-29; corresponds to Masoretic Psalm 102:1-22, 25-28

15 LXX Psalm 135; corresponds to Masoretic Psalm 136

16 Luke 12:37-38

17 Matthew 6:9-13

18 LXX Psalm 17:2-51; corresponds to Masoretic Psalm 18

19 LXX Psalm 43:2-27; corresponds to Masoretic Psalm 44

20 LXX Psalm 88:2-40, 43-44, 47-53; corresponds to Masoretic Psalm 89:1-39, 42-43, 46-52

21 LXX Psalm 118; corresponds to Masoretic Psalm 119

22 Matthew 14:25

23 LXX Psalm 68:2-27, 30-37; corresponds to Masoretic Psalm 69:1-26, 29-36

24 LXX Psalm 93; corresponds to Masoretic Psalm 94

25 LXX Psalm 103:1-4, 8-15, 20-35; corresponds to Masoretic Psalm 104:1-4, 8-15, 20-35

26 LXX Psalm 70; corresponds to Psalm 71

27 LXX Psalm 67:2, 8-11, 18-27, 29-36; corresponds to Masoretic Psalm 68:1-10, 17-26, 28-35

28 Ephesians 5:14

29 LXX Psalm 5:2-13; corresponds to Psalm 5:1-12

30 LXX Psalm 106: 1-2, 8-10, 21-22, 31-32; corresponds to Masoretic Psalm 107:1-2, 8-10, 21-22, 31-32

31 John 14:6

32 LXX Psalm 25; corresponds to Masoretic Psalm 26

33 Romans 11:33-36

34 LXX Psalm 99; corresponds to Masoretic Psalm 100

35 LXX Psalm 110; corresponds to Masoretic Psalm 111

36 Luke 1:68-69, 71-75, 78-79

37 I Peter 1:3; Ephesians 3:20-21
38 LXX Psalm 121:1; corresponds to Masoretic Psalm 122:1
39 Luke 11:2-4
40 LXX Psalm 131:8-11, 17-18; corresponds to Masoretic Psalm 132:8-18
41 Revelation 4:8b, 9b, 11
42 Matthew 5:3-10
43 LXX Psalm 26; corresponds to Masoretic Psalm 27
44 Romans 8.26
45 LXX Psalm 134:1-7, 13; corresponds to Masoretic Psalm 135:1-7, 13
46 I Corinthians 4:11-13
47 LXX Psalm 150; corresponds to Masoretic Psalm 150
48 Excerpts from Revelation 5:9-10, 12-13
49 I Peter 1:3; Romans 6:3; Mat 28:19b; John 14:16, 26; 15:26; 16:8; II Corinthians
        3:17; Romans 8:14a, 15b-17, 26
50 LXX Psalm 1; corresponds to Masoretic Psalm 1
51 Romans 10:9-10
52 Ephesians 4:4-6
53 LXX Isaiah 12:1b-2, 4b-6
54 LXX Isaiah 11:1-8, 10
55 Matthew 16:16b
56 Acts 4:24b-30
57 LXX Psalm 8:2-10; corresponds to Masoretic Psalm 8
58 Matthew 6:9-13
59 LXX Psalm 11:2-9; corresponds to Masoretic Psalm 12
60 LXX Psalm 19:2-10; corresponds to Masoretic Psalm 20
61 John 4:49
62 Colossians 3:15-17
63 LXX Psalm 113:22; corresponds to Masoretic Psalm 115:14
64 Romans 15:5-6, 13
65 II Corinthians 1:3-5
66 Galatians 6:18
67 John 6:68b-69
68 LXX Psalm 14:1-3; corresponds to Masoretic Psalm 15:1-3
69 Philippians 2:5b-11
70 LXX Psalm 15:1-2, 5-11; corresponds to Masoretic Psalm 16:1-2, 5-11
71 Revelation 7:12
72 LXX Psalm 4:2-9; corresponds to Masoretic Psalm 4
73 John 10:2-4, 11b
74 LXX Psalm 22; corresponds to Masoretic Psalm 23
75 II Corinthians 4:7-11
76 Ephesians 5:14
77 Ephesians 1:3-12
78 LXX Psalm 3:2-9; corresponds to Masoretic Psalm 3:1-8

79 Revelation 4:8b, 9b, 11

80 I Peter 1:3; Romans 6:3; Matthew 28:19b; John 14:16, 26; 15:26; 16:8; II Corinthians 3:17; Romans 8:14a, 15b-17, 26

81 LXX Psalm 33:2-6, 9-10, 19-21, 23; corresponds to Masoretic Psalm 34:1-5, 8-9, 18-20, 22

82 LXX Psalm 70:8; corresponds to Masoretic Psalm 71:8

83 John 1:1-5, 9-14, 16-17

84 LXX Psalm 18:8-15; corresponds to Masoretic Psalm 19:7-14

85 Colossians 1:12-20

86 LXX Psalm 20:2-9, 14; corresponds to Masoretic Psalm 21:1-8, 13

87 Philippians 3:8-10

88 LXX Psalm 126:1; corresponds to Masoretic Psalm 127:1

89 LXX Psalm 48:6-11, 16; corresponds to Masoretic Psalm 49:5-10, 15

90 Hebrews 1:1-3

91 LXX Psalm 35:6-12; corresponds to Masoretic Psalm 36:5-11

92 John 1:49; 11:27; 9:57

93 LXX Psalm 27; corresponds to Masoretic Psalm 28

94 LXX Psalm 28:1-2, 7-9, 11; corresponds to Masoretic Psalm 29:1-2, 7-9, 11

95 Hebrews 13:12-15

96 Revelation 1:5-6

97 LXX Isaiah 52:9 – 53:12

98 I Peter 1:3; Romans 6:3; Mat 28:19b; John 14:16, 26; 15:26; 16:8; II Corinthians 3:17; Romans 8:14a, 15b-17, 26

99 LXX Psalm 31:1-7, 10-11; corresponds to Masoretic Psalm 32:1-7, 10-11

100 Revelation 15:3b-4

101 LXX Psalm 32:20-22; corresponds to Masoretic Psalm 33:20-22

102 I John 5:1-12

103 LXX Psalm 38:2, 5-9, 13; corresponds to Masoretic Psalm 39:1, 4-8, 12

104 Ephesians 3:14-19

105 Matthew 5:3-10

106 LXX Psalm 120; corresponds to Masoretic Psalm 121

107 LXX Psalm 39:2-18; corresponds to Masoretic Psalm 40

108 LXX Psalm 42; corresponds to Masoretic Psalm 43

109 LXX Psalm 12:2-6; corresponds to Masoretic Psalm 13

110 Revelation 22:20b-21

111 LXX Psalm 16; corresponds to Masoretic Psalm 17

112 Ephesians 5:14

113 LXX Psalm 56:2-12; corresponds to Masoretic Psalm 57

114 LXX Psalm 7:2-3; 7-12; 18; corresponds to Masoretic Psalm 7:1-2, 6-11, 17

115 Romans 6:3b-10; Galatians 3:27

116 LXX Psalm 54: 2-10, 17-20; corresponds to Masoretic Psalm 55:1-9, 16-19

117 I Peter 1:3; Romans 6:3; Mat 28:19b; John 14:16, 26; 15:26; 16:8; II Corinthians 3:17; Romans 8:14a, 15b-17, 26

118 LXX Psalm 41:2-12; corresponds to Masoretic Psalm 42
119 Excerpts from Rev 19:4-6, 9
120 LXX Masoretic Psalm 44:2-18; corresponds to Masoretic Psalm 45
121 Jude 1:25
122 LXX Psalm 45:2-3, 8, 10-12; corresponds to Masoretic Psalm 46: 1-2, 7, 9-11
123 Revelation 7:12
124 LXX Psalm 91:2-16; corresponds to Masoretic Psalm 92:1-15
125 LXX Psalm 63: 2-3; corresponds to Masoretic Psalm 64:1-2
126 Revelation 15:3b-4
127 Matthew 6:9-13
128 LXX Psalm 34: 1-5, 10, 28; corresponds to Masoretic Psalm 35:1-5, 10, 28
129 Luke 1:46b-48a, 49-53
130 LXX Psalm 50:3-19; corresponds to Masoretic Psalm 51:1-17
131 LXX Psalm 47:2, 10-12, 15; corresponds to Masoretic Psalm 47:1, 9-11, 14
132 LXX Psalm 53:3-9; corresponds to Masoretic Psalm 54
133 II Corinthians 4:7-11
134 LXX Psalm 60:2-9; corresponds to Masoretic Psalm 61
135 John 6:68b-69
136 LXX Psalm 37:2-23; corresponds to Masoretic Psalm 38
137 I Peter 5:10-11
138 Colossians 1:9-20
139 LXX Psalm 19:2-3, 5-10; corresponds to Masoretic Psalm 20:1-2, 4-9
140 Romans 15:5-6, 13
141 LXX Psalm 58:2-5, 10, 17-18; corresponds to Masoretic Psalm 59:1-4, 9, 16-17
142 I Corinthians 4:11-13
143 LXX Psalm 61: 2-10, 12-13; corresponds to Masoretic Psalm 62:1-9, 11-12
144 LXX Psalm 59:3-7; 12-13; corresponds to Masoretic Psalm 60:1-5, 10-11
145 Revelation 4:8b, 9b, 11
146 LXX Psalm 62:2-12; corresponds to Masoretic Psalm 63
147 Ephesians 5:14
148 I Peter 1:3; Romans 6:3; Matthew 28:19b; excerpts of John 14:16, 26; 15:26;
        16:8; II Corinthians 3:16-18; Romans 5:3b-5; 8:14a, 15b-17, 26
149 LXX Psalm 69:2-6; corresponds to Masoretic Psalm 70:1-5
150 LXX Psalm 65; corresponds to Masoretic Psalm 66
151 Jude 1:25
152 Matthew 6:9-13
153 LXX Psalm 66:2-8; corresponds to Masoretic Psalm 67
154 Romans 11:33-36
155 LXX 72:1-3; 12-28; corresponds to Masoretic Psalm 73:1-3, 12-28
156 Revelation 1:5-6
157 LXX Ps 73:1-4; 7-8; 10-23; corresponds to Masoretic Ps 74:1-4, 7-8, 10-23
158 Revelation 4:8b, 11
159 LXX Psalm 75:2-13; corresponds to Masoretic Psalm 76:1-12

<u>End Notes</u>

---

160 Ephesians 1:3-12
161 LXX Psalm 102; corresponds to Masoretic Psalm 103
162 Romans 8:14a, 15b-17, 19, 22-23, 25-26
163 LXX Psalm 78:1-5, 8-11, 13; corresponds to Masoretic Psalm 79:1-5, 8-11, 13
164 Philippians 3:8-10
165 LXX Psalm 79:2-20; corresponds to Masoretic Psalm 80
166 Luke 6:20-23
167 Luke 9:38b-39
168 LXX Psalm 120; corresponds to Masoretic Psalm 121
169 Ephesians 3:14-19
170 I Peter 5:10-11
171 Matthew 5:3-10
172 LXX Psalm 84:2-14; corresponds to Masoretic Psalm 85
173 Revelation 15:3b-4
174 LXX Psalm 29:2-13; corresponds to Masoretic Psalm 30
175 LXX Psalm 87:2-7, 10, 14; corresponds to Masoretic Psalm 88:1-6, 11, 13
176 Ephesians 5:14
177 LXX Psalm 89; corresponds to Masoretic Psalm 90
178 LXX Psalm 126:1; corresponds to Masoretic Psalm 127:1
179 Revelation 4:8b, 9b, 11
180 Luke 2:14
181 I Corinthians 4:11-13
182 LXX Psalm 85; corresponds to Masoretic Psalm 86
183 Jude 1:25
184 Ephesians 4:4-6
185 Luke 5:12b; 17:13b; 18:38b, 39b
186 LXX Psalm 90; corresponds to Masoretic Psalm 91
187 I Timothy 2:1-4
188 Matthew 5:43-48
189 LXX Psalm 82:2-4, 17, 19; corresponds to Masoretic 83:1-3, 16, 18
190 LXX Psalm 92; corresponds to Masoretic Psalm 93
191 Galatians 3:27
192 I Timothy 1:17
193 I Peter 1:3; Romans 6:3; Mat 28:19b; John 14:16, 26; 15:26; 16:8; II Corinthians 3:17; Romans 8:14a, 15b-17, 26
194 LXX Psalm 140; corresponds to Masoretic Psalm 141
195 Jude 1:25
196 LXX Psalm 94; corresponds to Masoretic Psalm 95
197 Romans 6:3b-10
198 LXX Psalm 96:1, 8-9; corresponds to Masoretic Psalm 97:1, 8-9
199 I Timothy 3:16
200 LXX Psalm 95; corresponds to Masoretic Psalm 96
201 Revelation 11:17

End Notes

202 Excerpts from Revelation 5:9-10, 12-13
203 Revelation 22:20b-21
204 Luke 22:14-15
205 LXX Psalm 83:2-13; corresponds to Masoretic Psalm 84
206 LXX Psalm 97; corresponds to Masoretic Psalm 98
207 John 17:15, 17
208 Luke 23:34
209 Romans 15:5-6, 13
210 LXX Psalm 19:2-3, 5-10; corresponds to Masoretic Psalm 20:1-2, 4-9
211 Luke 6:20-23
212 LXX Numbers 6:24-26; corresponds to Masoretic Numbers 6:25-27
213 Luke 22:21
214 LXX Psalm 55:2-14; corresponds to Masoretic Psalm 56
215 LXX Psalm 98; corresponds to Masoretic Psalm 99
216 Luke 22:39-40
217 LXX Psalm 76:2-21; corresponds to Masoretic Psalm 77
218 Mark 14:40
219 LXX Psalm 40:2-14; corresponds to Masoretic Psalm 41
220 Luke 5:12b; 17:13b; 18:38b, 39b
221 LXX Psalm 125; corresponds to Masoretic Psalm 126
222 Ephesians 5:14
223 LXX Psalm 107:2-7, 13-14; corresponding to Masoretic Psalm 108:1-6, 12-13
224 I Peter 1:3; Romans 6:3; Matthew 28:19b; excerpts from John 14:16, 26; 15:26; 16:8; Romans 8:14a, 15b-17, 26
225 Jude 1:25
226 LXX Psalm 119; corresponds to Masoretic Psalm 120
227 LXX Psalm 105:1-7; 34-39, 47-48; corresponds to Masoretic Psalm 106:1-7, 34-39, 47-48
228 Mark 15:25-26
229 LXX Psalm 71:1-19; corresponds to Masoretic Psalm 72
230 LXX Psalm 116; corresponds to Masoretic Psalm 117
231 LXX Psalm 30:2-25; corresponds to Masoretic Psalm 31
232 LXX Psalm 114:1-9; corresponds to Masoretic Psalm 116:1-9
233 Luke 5:12; 9:57; 17:13b; 18:38b, 39b
234 LXX Psalm 115:1-4, 6-10, where 115:5 would repeat 115:9 if that verse were used twice in the LXX as the Masoretes repeated it; corresponds to Masoretic Psalm 116:10-19
235 John 19:14-15
236 LXX Psalm 109:1-7; corresponds to Masoretic Psalm 110
237 LXX Psalm 64:2-14; corresponds to Masoretic Psalm 65
238 John 1:49; 12:13; Luke 19:38; 23:42b
239 Matthew 27:45
240 Philippians 2:5b-11

---

241 LXX 108:1-5, 21-31;corresponds to Masoretic Psalm 109:1-5, 21-31

242 I Peter 1:3; Romans 6:3; Mat 28:19b; John 14:16, 26; 15:26; 16:8; II Corinthians 3:17; Romans 8:14a, 15b-17, 26

243 LXX Psalm 123; corresponds to Masoretic Psalm 124

244 Revelation 4:8b, 9b, 11

245 Matthew 27:46

246 LXX Psalm 113:9-26; corresponds to Masoretic Psalm 115:1-18

247 Excerpts from Revelation 5:9-10, 12-13

248 Luke 22:32

249 II Thessalonians 2:16-17

250 Luke 6:20-23

251 LXX Psalm 120; corresponds to Masoretic Psalm 121

252 I Thessalonians 3:11-13

253 I Thessalonians 5:23-24, 28

254 LXX Psalm 117:1, 4-9, 13-29; corresponds to Masoretic Psalm 118:1,4-9,13-29

255 LXX Psalm 6:2-11; corresponds to Masoretic Psalm 6:1-10

256 LXX Psalm 133; corresponds to Masoretic Psalm 134

257 LXX Psalm 129; corresponds to Masoretic Psalm 130

258 Ephesians 5:14

259 I Peter 1:3; Romans 6:3; Matthew 28:19b; John 14:16, 26; 15:26; 16:8; II Corinthians 3:17; Romans 8:14a, 15b-17, 26

260 LXX Psalm 130; corresponds to Masoretic Psalm 131

261 I Corinthians 4:11-13

262 Revelation 1:5-6

263 LXX Psalm 112; corresponds to Masoretic Psalm 113

264 Matthew 6:9-13

265 LXX Psalm 137; corresponds to Masoretic Psalm 138

266 LXX Psalm 139:2-9, 13-14; corresponds to Masoretic Psalm 140:1-8, 12-13

267 LXX Psalm 146; corresponds to Masoretic Psalm 147

268 LXX Psalm 24; corresponds to Masoretic Psalm 25

269 Psalm 141:2-8; corresponds to Masoretic Psalm 142

270 Jude 1:25

271 LXX Psalm 148; corresponds to Masoretic Psalm 148

272 John 1:49; Matthew 14:33b; 16:16b; John 11:27; Luke 9:57; 17:10b; John 6:68b-69

273 LXX Psalm 143:1, 3-15; corresponds to Masoretic Psalm 144:1, 3-15

274 LXX Psalm 144; corresponds to Masoretic Psalm 145, but with an additional verse (13a) in the LXX

275 Luke 1:46b-48a, 49-53

276 LXX Psalm 147:1-4, 8-9; corresponds to Masoretic Psalm 147:12-15, 19-20

277 Matthew 5:3-10

278 I Peter 1:3; Romans 6:3; Mat 28:19b; John 14:16, 26; 15:26; 16:8; II Corinthians 3:17; Romans 8:14a, 15b-17, 26

---

279 LXX Psalm 145; corresponds to Masoretic Psalm 146
280 Hebrews 13:20-21
281 LXX Psalm 19:2-3, 5-10; corresponds to Masoretic Psalm 20:1-2, 4-9
282 Colossians 1:9-20
283 Revelation 15:3b-4
284 LXX Psalm 138:1-18, 23-24; corresponds to Masoretic Psalm 139:1-18, 23-24
285 LXX Psalm 122; corresponds to Masoretic Psalm 123
286 LXX Psalm 142; corresponds to Masoretic Psalm 143
287 LXX Psalm 149:1-5; corresponds to Masoretic Psalm 149:1-5
288 John 6:51, 53b-58, 63
289 I Corinthians 11:22-29
290 Jeremiah 38:31-33; Ezekiel 36:26-27; corresponds to Masoretic Jeremiah
         31:31-33; Ezekiel 36:26-27
291 Matthew 26:26-32
292 Luke 24:13, 15-17, 19b-20, 25-27, 30-31
293 Acts 2:40-47
294 I Corinthians 10:1-6, 16-17
295 Matthew 20:17-23; Mt 27:36-37
296 LXX Isaiah 53:1-3